BEATRIX POTTER'S **LAKE DISTRICT**

BEATRIX POTTER'S **LAKE DISTRICT**

Gilly Cameron Cooper

Foreword by Fiona Reynolds,
Director General of the National Trust

With photographs from the National Trust Photo Library

FREDERICK WARNE

FREDERICK WARNE

Published by the Penguin Group
Penguin Books Ltd, 80 Strand, London WC2R 0RL, England
Penguin Group (USA) Inc., 375 Hudson Street, New York, New York 10014, USA
Penguin Group (Canada), 90 Eglinton Avenue East, Suite 700, Toronto, Ontario, Canada M4P 2Y3
Penguin Ireland, 25 St Stephen's Green, Dublin 2, Ireland
Penguin (Group) Australia, 250 Camberwell Road, Camberwell, Victoria 3124, Australia
Penguin Books India (P) Ltd, 11 Community Centre, Panchsheel Park, New Delhi 110 017, India
Penguin Group (NZ), 67 Apollo Drive, Rosedale, North Shore 0632, New Zealand
(a division of Pearson New Zealand Ltd)
Penguin Books (South Africa) (Pty) Ltd, P O Box 9, Parklands 2121, South Africa

Penguin Books Ltd, Registered Offices: 80 Strand, London WC2R 0RL, England

Web site at: www.peterrabbit.com

First published by Frederick Warne 2007
1 3 5 7 9 10 8 6 4 2
New reproductions of Beatrix Potter's book illustrations copyright © Frederick Warne & Co., 2002
Original text and illustrations copyright © Frederick Warne & Co., 1903, 1905, 1906, 1907, 1908,
1909, 1913, 1918, 1929

Frederick Warne & Co. is the owner of all rights, copyrights and trademarks in the
Beatrix Potter character names and illustrations.

ISBN 978 0 7232 5853 7

Design by Perfect Bound Ltd

Printed and bound in Singapore

Photograph previous page: Great Langdale
Opposite: Slater Bridge in Little Langdale
Next page: Hawse End landing stage, Derwentwater

CONTENTS

Foreword

Fiona Reynolds
Director General of the National Trust

Inspired by the Lake District, its beauty and the farming which created it, Beatrix Potter spent the last thirty years of her life protecting as much land as possible. Her vision of people and place in harmony was combined with an immensely practical and pragmatic approach to life, and these sentiments remain constant in our approach to the Lake District today.

Beatrix's remarkable ability to draw and tell stories, and to capture the personality and mood of a landscape and its creatures, surprised many who knew her as a quiet young woman. But through these talents she awoke an even deeper love – for a way of life that was fast disappearing; vernacular architecture and furniture; and the tough life of hill farmers and their sheep and the extraordinary landscape they created together.

She wanted these to continue – not out of sentimentality – but because she believed they contributed something vital to human experience. And thanks to the confidence she and others like her placed in the National Trust we are able to continue these traditions today.

As these beautiful pictures show, our task is no small one: to sustain the essence of these inspiring landscapes while ensuring they are still living, working places where people can earn a living and communities can thrive; and where visitors can enjoy the sense of freedom, space and astonishing beauty of a land immortalised by artists and poets for the past four hundred years. This does not mean that nothing changes: rather, as Beatrix herself recognised, it means managing change in ways that are consistent with the spirit of the place. Beatrix herself described 'the difficulty of reconciling ancient relics and modern sanitation' and, with additional pressures like climate change, it is even more challenging today.

Visitors to Hill Top today see Beatrix's life and work as an author and artist. This homely and evocative farmhouse, together with the landscape and farms beyond, are nurtured by the Trust as a permanent memorial to her talent and vision, and a living example of what can be achieved through dedication and commitment and a strong dose of practicality.

Beatrix worked tirelessly to save the land for future generations as best she could: sometimes buying it herself; often contributing anonymously to appeals. Her response to thanks was simple:

Those of us who have felt the spirit of the fells reckon little of passing praise; but I do value the esteem of others who have

understanding. It seems that we have done a big thing; without premeditation; suddenly; inevitably – what else could one do? It will be a happy consummation if the Trust is able to turn this quixotic venture into a splendid reality.'
Letter to John Bailey Feb 1930

What else could one do indeed? If, over seventy years later, there was any doubt as to the relevance of this statement, then the Trust's 3.5 million members, whose generosity enables us to continue turning the protection of our nation's heritage into a 'splendid reality', goes some way to providing the answer.

Above: Brandelhow Park, on the westward shores of Derwentwater, was the result of the National Trust's first major appeal for funds to buy land, in 1902.

Left: The front cover illustration for *The Tale of Squirrel Nutkin.*

Map of locations

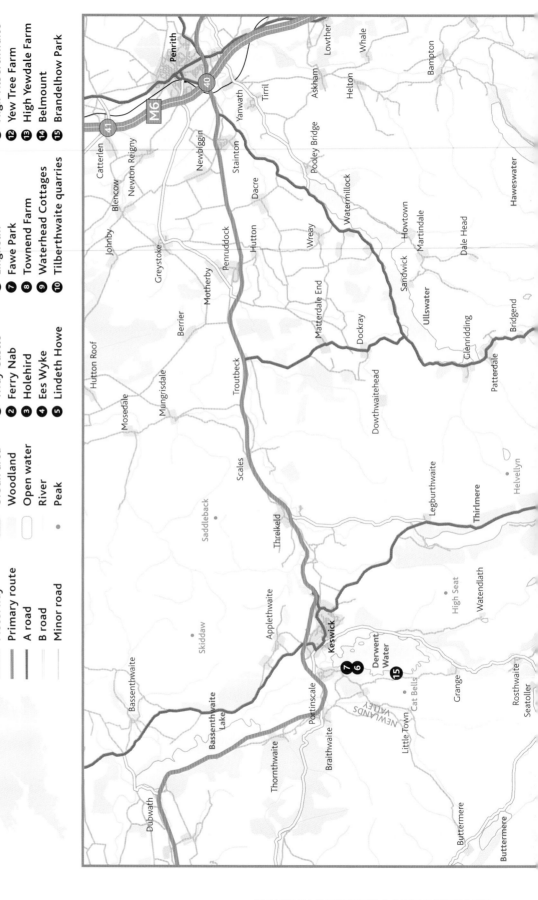

Motorway
Primary route
A road
B road
Minor road

Urban area
Woodland
Open water
River
Peak

1 Wray Castle
2 Ferry Nab
3 Holehird
4 Ees Wyke
5 Lindeth Howe

6 Lingholm
7 Fawe Park
8 Townend Farm
9 Waterhead Cottages
10 Tilberthwaite quarries

11 High Tilberthwaite
12 Yew Tree Farm
13 High Yewdale Farm
14 Belmount
15 Brandelhow Park

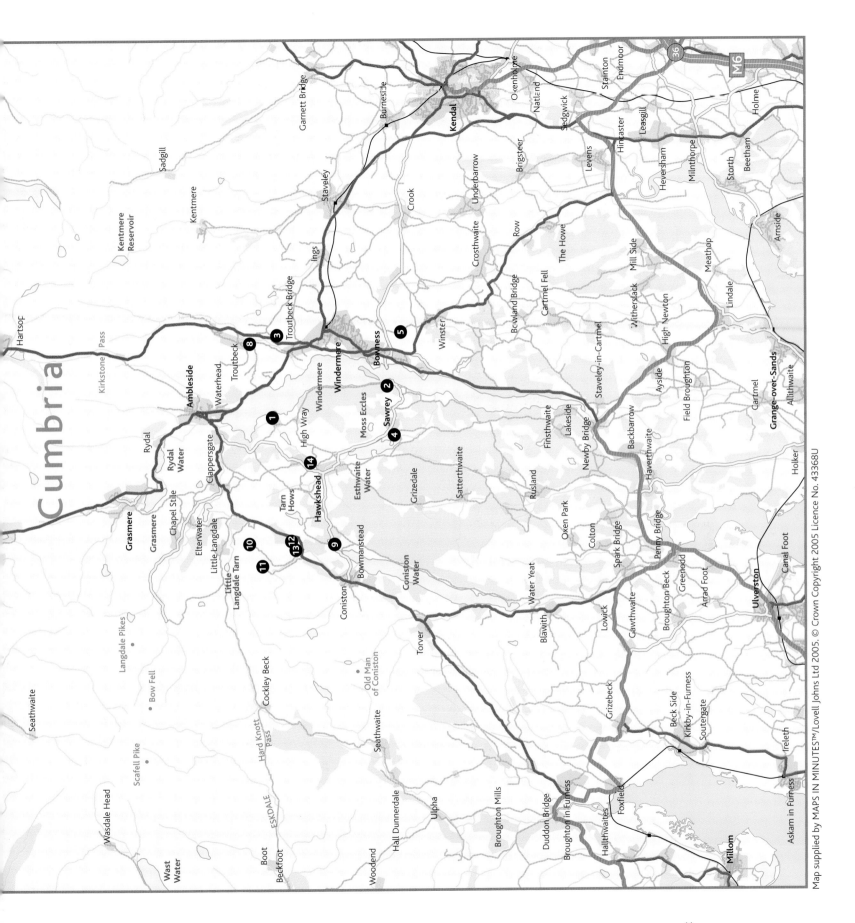

Cumbria

Hartsop

Kirkstone Pass

Seathwaite

Wasdale Head

Scafell Pike

Bow Fell

Langdale Pikes

Wast Water

Boot

Beckfoot

ESKDALE

Cockley Beck

Hard Knott Pass

Seathwaite

Woodend

Hall Dunnerdale

Ulpha

Broughton Mills

Duddon Bridge

Broughton in Furness

Hallthwaites

Foxfield

Millom

Askam in Furness

Grasmere

Rydal

Grasmere

Chapel Stile

Rydal Water

Elterwater

Little Langdale

Little Langdale Tarn

Ambleside

Clappersgate

Waterhead

Troutbeck

Coniston

Torver

Blawith

Water Yeat

Lowick

Gawthwaite

Beck Side

Grizebeck

Kirkby-in-Furness

Soutergate

Ireleth

Old Man of Coniston

Coniston Water

Bowmanstead

Tarn Hows

Hawkshead

Grizedale

Esthwaite Water

Satterthwaite

Rusland

Oxen Park

Colton

Spark Bridge

Broughton Beck

Greenodd

Arrad Foot

Penny Bridge

Ulverston

Canal Foot

Holker

Backbarrow

Haverthwaite

Field Broughton

Cartmel

Allithwaite

Grange-over-Sands

High Wray

Windermere

Moss Eccles

Sawrey

Windermere

Bowness

Troutbeck

Troutbeck Bridge

Ings

Staveley

Garnett Bridge

Burneside

Kendal

Oxenholme

Natland

Sedgwick

Brigsteer

Underbarrow

Crosthwaite

Crook

Winster

Row

The Howe

Bowland Bridge

Cartmel Fell

Witherslack

High Newton

Staveley-in-Cartmel

Ayside

Lindale

Meathop

Levens

Heversham

Hincaster

Leasgill

Milnthorpe

Storth

Arnside

Beetham

Holme

Stainton

Endmoor

Mill Side

Finsthwaite

Lakeside

Newby Bridge

Sadgill

Kentmere Reservoir

Kentmere

Waterhead

M6

36

1 2 3 4 5 8 9 10 11 12 13 14

Map supplied by MAPS IN MINUTES™/Lovell Johns Ltd 2005. © Crown Copyright 2005 Licence No. 43368U

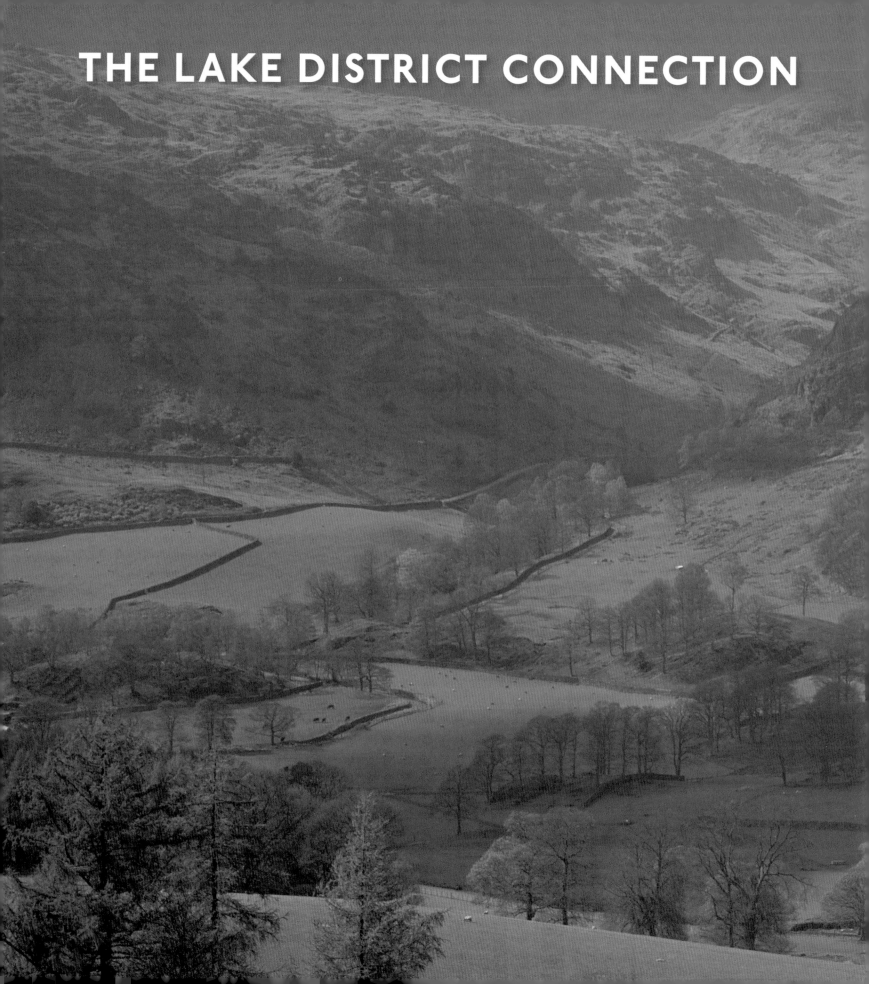

THE LAKE DISTRICT CONNECTION

The Lake District connection

'My brother and I were born in London because my father was a lawyer there. But our descent – our interests and our joy was in the north country,' Beatrix Potter wrote. The families of both her parents had prospered in the Lancashire cotton industry, which boomed in the nineteenth century with the new machines of the Industrial Revolution. Like many industrial barons of the north, Beatrix's great-grandfather, Abraham Crompton, had invested in land in the Lake District, land that Beatrix was to buy back towards the end of her life. But during her younger days, the Lake District was where she spent family holidays, and where many of the tales that made her enduringly famous, were set and written.

If you visit certain parts of the Lake District today, you can walk into the world and life of Beatrix Potter and into the illustrated pages of the little books. You can stroll into the farmyard where Jemima Puddle-duck laid her eggs, climb the fells to visit Mrs Tiggy-winkle, and stop by the wall where Tom Kitten and his sisters liked to sit.

The Lake District landscapes most popularly associated with Beatrix Potter are the homely rural scenes that appear in her books rather than the large-scale operatic stage sets of the surrounding fells. The grandeur of the mountains contain and emphasize these little worlds. But Beatrix was much more than the author of the tales, and her Lakeland a much broader canvas than that depicted in them.

The enduring appeal of her illustrated tales has ensured the preservation of many favourite Lake District scenes on paper. But Beatrix Potter made sure they were preserved in actuality, by buying vast tracts of land and many traditional buildings and leaving them to the nation on her death, with strict instructions on how they should be conserved.

The Lake District ultimately became her home, and Beatrix embraced the traditional rural lifestyle, becoming a respected and successful farmer and landowner, and marrying into the local community. Little by little, Beatrix Potter, author and illustrator, was left behind. Today, it is as Mrs William Heelis, farmer and conservationist, that she is remembered with respect by the local country people.

Above: A corner of the third-floor school room at 2 Bolton Gardens, drawn by Beatrix in 1885. On the hearth-rug is a terrapin.

Right: Beatrix, her father, her brother Bertram, her mother and the dog, Spot, on holiday at Dalguise House in Scotland in 1881.

Beatrix's life falls into three parts: her early years living in London with her parents, her working career as a writer when she started to buy property of her own, and finally the period after her marriage. Each section marks a deeper involvement with the Lake District.

She was born in July 1866, in a newly built house in Bolton Gardens, Kensington, then a peaceful, leafy suburb of London. Her father, Rupert Potter, came from a wealthy Lancashire cotton family, the new 'middle' class that had made its money on the back of the Industrial Revolution. He was a barrister, but led a leisurely life mixing with friends, politicians and literati, and becoming an accomplished photographer. He introduced Beatrix to a wider world, taking her to art galleries and exhibitions, and to visit distinguished friends, such as the artist John Millais.

Her mother Helen's life revolved round taking tea with lady friends, and organizing the household. Her retinue of servants – cook, housekeeper, butler, coachman, groom, plus nurses and governesses – confirmed the family's comfortable middle-class status.

Beatrix had one brother, Bertram, who was six years younger than she was. Despite the age gap, they were close friends and shared a love of the countryside, animals and drawing.

Beatrix was brought up in a manner appropriate to her middle-class Victorian background. She was cared for by a nanny, with minimal parental contact in the early years, and educated at home by governesses. Fortunately, however, her parents encouraged her to develop her artistic talent and were tolerant of her enthusiasm for natural history. She and Bertram kept all

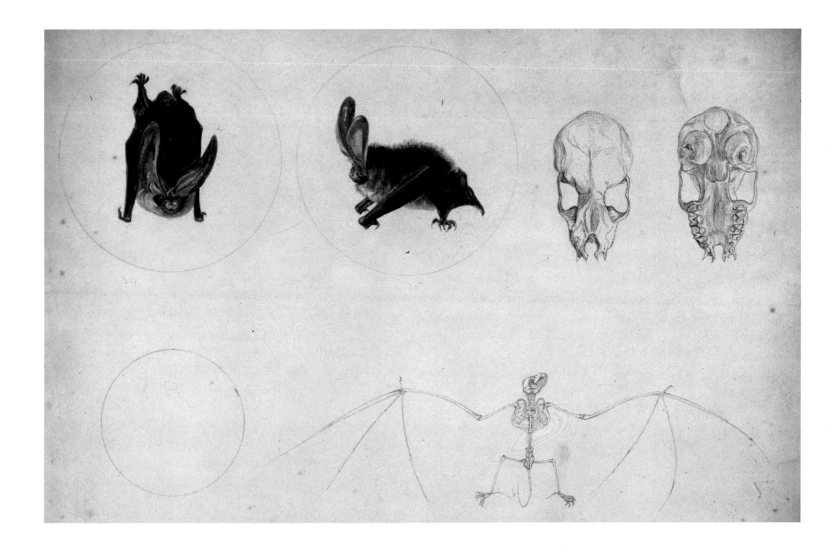

Above: Beatrix's study of a bat, including drawings of the skull and a bat skeleton, dated 1887.

kinds of creatures in the school room at Bolton Gardens, including rabbits, mice, lizards, a snake, a bat and a frog. On holiday in the country they caught wild rabbits and tamed them. They skinned and boiled dead animals and spent hours studying and drawing the skeletons. The journal Beatrix wrote in code from the age of fifteen reveals a sensitive, curious and observant young girl.

Every summer, the Potters decamped – pets, servants and all – for three months' holiday in the country. When Beatrix was a child their most popular holiday home was Dalguise House, in the Tay Valley, Scotland. For Beatrix the eleven summers spent at Dalguise acted as a prelude to her later deep involvement with the Lake District countryside. Here she was able to explore the countryside and study its wildlife.

The Potter family took the first of their summer holidays in the Lake District in 1882 when Beatrix was sixteen. From then on it became a regular summer destination.

With its unique land formations, mild, damp climate and unpolluted atmosphere, the area was fertile ground for a girl like the young Beatrix, who was deeply interested in natural history. She explored with her sketchbook and paints, absorbing the moods and secrets of the countryside, from the miniature worlds of fungus and fossils to the sky-sweeping fells. She was a great observer and recorded what she saw in moody watercolours of landscapes and meticulous botanical studies.

Above left: One of Beatrix's Christmas card designs for the firm of Hildesheimer & Faulkner, 1890.

Above right: Beatrix Potter and William Heelis at the time of their wedding in October 1913.

Opposite: Beatrix with a sheepdog outside her home, Castle Farm, in about 1930.

However Beatrix also enjoyed producing fantasy drawings of animals in imaginary situations. In 1890, at the age of twenty-three, she started selling drawings for greetings cards. Her pet rabbit, Benjamin Bouncer, was the model for her first published pictures, which appeared as Christmas and New Year's cards. This creative aspect of her work was eventually to lead her to a career as a children's book author. She had remained great friends with the last of her governesses, Annie Carter, later Mrs Annie Moore, and Beatrix practised her storytelling skills on Annie's children. One particular story, which started life as a letter to Annie's elder son, Noel, became Beatrix's very first published book, *The Tale of Peter Rabbit*.

With the publication of *The Tale of Peter Rabbit* by the London firm of Frederick Warne & Co. in 1902, the most productive period of Beatrix's life as an artist and writer began. Between 1902 and 1917 she produced twenty of her famous twenty-three tales. With the income from her books she was able to fulfil her dream of buying property in the Lake District. Increasingly her tales were placed in Lake District settings.

In 1913 Beatrix married Cumbrian solicitor William Heelis and she was at last able to focus almost all of her life on the Lake District. Up till that point her parents had demanded that their unmarried daughter continue to look after their needs and run the family household in London. But as Mrs Beatrix Heelis, she was able to settle into her new roles as countrywoman and wife, farmer, conservationist and landowner.

WINDERMERE

Windermere:
Beatrix's introduction to the Lake District

Every year, from around mid-July to mid-October, the Potter family shut up their London house, and, with children, servants and pets, headed for the country. For many years they went to Scotland, but in 1882 the Scottish let was unavailable, so they took advantage of family connections and moved to the Lake District. Many industrial barons like Beatrix's great-grandfather, Abraham Crompton, who had made their money from Lancashire cotton mills and other industries born of the Industrial Revolution, bought country estates in the neighbouring beauty spot of the English Lakes. The area was close and fashionable, a convenient escape from the noise, grime and workers of their factories, and somewhere they could mix with their social equals. The Lake District's popularity as a desirable destination for artists and poets, and the patronage of the northern industrialists, ensured that this north-west extremity of England kept abreast of the times. The nouveau riche of the north built big houses in the latest styles to show off their wealth and status, fitting them with the latest gadgets and inventions, such as flush toilets, and furnishing the rooms with drapes and carpets from the new power looms. The houses lay empty for much of the year and could be let out to respectable people like the Potters.

Over the second half of the nineteenth century, the tentacles of the public railway network reached into ever-more distant corners of Britain, a direct line from London Euston connecting to Windermere as early as 1847. The journey took the Potters eight to ten hours by train in the 1880s, and breakdowns were frequent. But stretching ahead of them were six to eight weeks of country air. Their first Lake District holiday, on the north-western shore of Windermere, was clearly a success, and many summers in the area followed.

The Potters' rather grand holiday lets on the east and west shores of Windermere enjoyed vistas through parkland down to the lake. The slimly tapering body of water reflected the mood of the seasons and was framed by England's highest mountains. The lake was also the focal point of everyday life and leisure. The most passable roads clung to the lake shores and, although they were carrying horse-drawn vehicles well into the twentieth century, they still follow more or less the same routes today. In those days, though, it was often quicker and more reliable to travel on one of the steam ferries that plied the lake from Waterhead near Ambleside or Bowness to the western side of the lake. Tourism was already well established, and once the railway had come to Windermere and Lakeside, the lake buzzed with day-trippers and long-term holidaymakers messing about in sailing boats and rowing boats, fishing, bathing and sight-seeing.

It was in her explorations around Windermere that Beatrix discovered Sawrey, a village set back a little from the central western shores, where she would eventually live.

The Potter's first holiday home in the Lake District in 1882 was Wray Castle, a neo-gothic folly of a house on the north-western shores of Lake Windermere. Massive and top-heavy with deeply crenellated towers, it was built by a Liverpool surgeon, with, Beatrix reported in her journal 'his wife's money. Her father Robert Preston made gin; that was where the money came from . . . It took seven years to finish. The stone was brought across the lake. One old horse dragged it all up to the house on a kind of tram way. The architect killed himself with drinking before the house was finished.'

Inside living rooms and bedrooms range around a central well, baronial in its dark, gloomy heights that rise in dizzying perspective past panelled and balustraded landings to a distant oak-raftered pinnacle. But throw open the shutters of the eastern downstairs rooms, where gothic turrets provide extra bulges in order to squeeze in as many windows as possible, and eye and soul fly into light and space, over the lake to the fells.

With its mix of wild mountains, fields and woodlands, lake and shore, it was a perfect place for Beatrix to explore, observe birds and flowers, and paint.

Left: Looking across Windermere towards Wray Castle.

Below: Beatrix rows friends and family ashore in this photograph from the 1882 Windermere holiday.

BEATRIX POTTER'S **LAKE DISTRICT**

Wray Castle Latitude 54:23:59N Longitude 2:57:50W Landranger map reference NY375008

On a clear day with a bracing breeze, the Potters would look through the high windows of their holiday home and see a glittering expanse flagged with the wind-swollen white triangles of Class 1 Windermere yachts, which were enjoying their heyday in the 1880s. The 22 foot long, lead-keeled boats weighed $3^1/_2$ tons, and the sails of today's nearest equivalent have but a third of the sail area.

Rowing was also a popular pastime on Windermere. The general public could hire boats (on every day but Sunday) but the Potters probably used one that came with the house.

Rupert Potter was an enthusiastic fisherman and Windermere had a plentiful supply of fish including charr, a Lake District speciality. This freshwater member of the salmon family is a relic from the Ice Age and is there still: a dry, white, mild-flavoured fish.

Right: Wray Castle library, painted by Beatrix in 1882, is, like the rest of the house, an extravagance of burnished wood and fashionable Gothic Revival features, bossed, finialled and chunkily carved.

The boathouse at Wray Castle recalls the Traitors' Gate in the Tower of London; all that is missing is a portcullis. Several boats can be moored within its covered and outer pool. The Potters probably had the use of the Castle's private steamboat during their stay, and, like neighbouring families, sent their housekeeper with the boatman to Bowness to take the laundry and collect provisions. Alternatively, they could use the service provided by steamboats like the *Raven*, which collected farm produce and delivered provisions on a twenty-two-mile round trip of the lakeside settlements from 1871 to 1920. It was fast service, too. In those days, a boat could literally steam along at 25 mph; today the limit is 10 mph.

In the late 1800s, you could take your own horse-drawn gig or the public coach across on the ferry from Bowness to the western side of the lake. 'On calm summer waters no voyage is more cheerful and pleasant than this crossing of Windermere,' Beatrix wrote.

Today a vehicle and passenger ferry still operates from Ferry Nab (headland) at Bowness across the lake. Bowness, just south of Windermere town, lies in a green bowl in the steep hills that fall to the lake shore. It is the older of the two settlements and started life as a fishing village. By the time the Potters visited the area, Bowness was already established as a lakeside pleasure resort for day trippers from the northern mills.

Opposite top: A view over the gentle landscape west of Windermere.

Opposite bottom: Rupert Potter took this photograph of Beatrix driving her carriage along a Lakeland road in 1889.

While the Potters were staying at Wray Castle they met the owner's cousin, Canon Hardwicke Rawnsley, athlete, poet, and at that time vicar of Wray. He was then in his early 30s, passionate about the Lake District, interested in geology and natural history, and most significantly, as far as his influence on Beatrix was concerned, an active conservationist. In 1895, he, together with Octavia Hill and Robert Hunter, formed the National Trust 'to act as general trustees for all property intended for the use and enjoyment of the nation at large'.

Beatrix and Canon Rawnsley remained life-long friends. He assisted her in finding a publisher for her first book, *The Tale of Peter Rabbit*, and his views on conservation and the environment were a permanent inspiration to her.

In the days before cars, Beatrix explored the lanes around the lake in a horse and trap. She got to know the low, rolling countryside inland of the western shores of Lake Windermere, where there are patches of woodland with trees well spaced, and light filtering through to earthy, grassy avenues, bordered in spring and summer by wild flowers – the world of Timmy Tiptoes and Mr Tod.

The photograph above is typical of the scenery west of Windermere, with High Loanthwaite Farm, which Beatrix was to own in later years, set in a pocket of miniature landscape, far removed from the bustle of the lake just over the hill, and the wild fell known as the Old Man of Coniston in the distance.

Hawkshead Latitude 54:22:27N Longitude 2:59:49W Landranger map reference SD353981

When the Potters were staying at Wray, their nearest market town was Hawkshead. An ancient settlement, Hawkshead was so-named because it was the summer pasture of Haukr, a Norseman who laid claim to the land following the influx of Nordic settlers in the tenth century. Now a cluster of lime-washed houses nestling in the hills beneath Monk Coniston Moor, it has changed little in its layout and charm.

Beatrix had clearly not developed her country legs when she described a cross-country walk from Wray to Hawkshead: 'Inquired the way three times, lost continually, alarmed by collies at every farm, stuck in stiles, chased once by cows.'

Opposite: View over Hawkshead.

Above: The approach to Hawkshead, sketched by Beatrix.

Left: This illustration from *The Tale of Johnny Town-Mouse* shows a covered alleyway in Hawkshead. Though the book was published in 1917, when motor cars had been on the roads for several years, in this story the streets of Hawkshead still rumble with carts.

Holehird Latitude 54:23:56N Longitude 2:54:51W Landranger map reference NY407007

In 1889 and again in 1895 the Potters rented Holehird, another Victorian pile, on the opposite shore of Lake Windermere to Wray. The rambling, heavily gabled, neo-gothic edifice of the 1860s might not have been quite to Beatrix's taste – she later wrote, when staying in a much smaller house: 'I think myself that a house that is too small is more comfortable than one a great deal too large . . .' The house's situation, though, commands a panorama of lake and fells that is breathtaking in its drama and distances. Many years later, Beatrix bought much of the land that you can see across the lake, as well as land on Coniston Fell itself, and in the Troutbeck Valley which reaches into the fells beyond Holehird. Today, Holehird is a Cheshire Home and Royal Horticultural Society Garden.

Ees Wyke Latitude 54:21:11 N Longitude 2:58:27 W Landranger map reference SD367957

Lakefield (also known as Ees Wyke), where the Potters stayed in 1896 and 1902, was a little inland from the west shore of Windermere. It was on the edge of the village of Sawrey, a village which Beatrix fell in love with, and where she would settle many years later. She described it in a letter to Noel Moore, the son of Annie Moore, her old governess: 'It is nearly as perfect a little place as I ever lived in, and such nice old-fashioned people in the village.'

In the watercolours Beatrix painted at Lakefield she set the luxuriant, enclosed world of the garden against the gentle farmed landscape, and, in the distance, the wild fells.

Lindeth Howe Latitude 54:20:59N Longitude 2:55:26W Landranger map reference SD400952

Above: Lindeth Howe.

Right: Bearded lichen festoons a tree at Lindeth Howe, an indication that the atmosphere is moist and unpolluted. Beatrix had cultivated and studied the spores of lichen as a young woman; her theory – that lichen is a combination of fungus and algae – was later proved correct.

On the hillside that rises steeply from the eastern shores of Lake Windermere, just south of Bowness, is Lindeth Howe, built in a 28-acre estate by another wealthy mill owner in the 1870s. The garden drops steeply through larch and rhododendron, birch and pine to the eastern shores of the lake and the requisite panorama over the lake to the south-west. Beatrix spent her last holiday as a single woman with her parents here in the summer of 1913, before marrying William Heelis in October. A year later, Rupert Potter died, and five years after that, Beatrix persuaded her mother to move to the Lake District. For the rest of her life Helen Potter, Beatrix's 'rather imperious old mother', lived at Lindeth Howe, with four maids, two gardeners and a driver, cages of canaries and a dog called Betty.

Left: Maids, gardeners and the chauffeur who worked for Mrs Potter at Lindeth Howe in about 1920.

Below: Mr Potter, Bertram and Beatrix at Lindeth Howe in August 1911.

Above: Looking south across Windermere from Cockshott Point.

Left: Looking west from Cockshott Point to Belle Isle, an island in Windermere.

Opposite: Early morning mist over Windermere, photographed from Cockshott Point.

Windermere was Beatrix's introduction to the Lake District and it always remained close to her heart. In 1927, she appealed on behalf of the National Trust to the American fans of her books to save a 'strip of foreshore woodland and meadow near Windermere Ferry from imminent risk of disfigurement by extensive building.' So, thanks to Beatrix, you can now stroll from Bowness marina to Cockshott Point, an open, grassy spot of land that juts into the lake, and gaze to the mountain rim north and west, and far to the wooded south.

Holidays at Derwentwater

Derwentwater, some twelve miles to the northwest of Windermere, fills a wide vale that stretches north from the central dome of the Lake District. The contrast between scarred mountain and soft, green, secret valleys is never so sharp as here. The eastern shores of the lake hug the feet of abruptly rising crags, while little villages nestle charmingly in pockets of brook-fed lowland between the flanking fells of Borrowdale to the south, and Derwent fells to the west. When Beatrix was in her twenties and thirties, the Potters spent many summer holidays in country houses set among parkland and woods that cascade down to the north-western shores of the lake.

The Derwentwater holidays coincided with the period when Beatrix wrote the first of her little books. Many were set in and inspired by the countryside around her. Benjamin Bunny's adventures took place in a Derwentwater garden, Squirrel Nutkin sailed from the lake shore beneath the Potter holiday homes to cock a snook at the resident owl on St Herbert's Island, and Mrs Tiggy-winkle lived in the nearby Newlands Valley.

Although, as time passed, Beatrix admitted that she sometimes found the family holiday 'a weary business', she was always able to escape into the valleys and hillsides with her sketch-pad and paints.

Above, left and previous page: The wide expanse of Derwentwater has a more intimate and contained atmosphere than Windermere, a squat 3 miles by 1 mile compared with Windermere's skinny 10½ by 1¼ miles. It is also only a third as deep.

DERWENTWATER

Keswick Latitude 54:35:57N Longitude 3:07:33W Landranger map reference NY273232

Keswick, the largest town in the Lake District National Park, lies in the flat plain between the fells north of Derwentwater, just a few miles from where the Potters holidayed on the north-western shores of the lake. Even today the car journey from Sawrey to Keswick takes over an hour. The road follows the route she would have taken, fitting tightly into a narrow, winding ledge beside the dark waters of Thirlmere, then rising towards a giant, U-shaped cross-section of a glaciated valley, like a portal to the northern lakes. It then escapes from the valley confines and sweeps over one of the ridges that fans out from the Lake District's central dome before dropping to Keswick in a wide meltwater plain.

Opposite: Looking down to Derwentwater, with Keswick on the flat plain between the fells.

Above: The broad vale of Derwentwater could not have been moulded by the narrow ribbon of a stream that threads its way down to the lake today, but by the far greater volume of a glacier and its meltwater.

Left: Thirlmere, on the route from Lake Windermere to Keswick.

DERWENTWATER

Right: Moot Hall and Keswick market in the early twentieth century.

Below: Beatrix's pencil sketches of Keswick railway station and market stalls.

Opposite: A view across Derwentwater to Keswick, with Blencathra in the background.

Coming from London, the Potters would have travelled to Keswick by train (the Penrith–Keswick–Cockermouth line had opened in 1865), accompanied by Beatrix's pets, including one of the stars of the Derwentwater-inspired tales, hedgehog Mrs Tiggy-winkle in a basket. 'She enjoys going by train, she is always very hungry when she is on a journey.'

When the Potters stayed at Derwentwater, Keswick was their nearest town. Beatrix sketched the Saturday market scene in 1903. Moot Hall in the centre of Market Square now houses the tourist information office. She was clearly much happier in the countryside, describing the town as 'awfully dull'. It 'pulls me down in August,' she wrote to an American friend, 'though quite delightful in autumn when there is a bit of frost'.

BEATRIX POTTER'S **LAKE DISTRICT**

Lingholm Latitude 54:35:24N Longitude 3:09:21W Landranger map reference NY254222

The house that the Potters used most frequently as a holiday home in the Derwentwater area was Lingholm, another property from the wave of country-house building by northern industrialists in the Lake District. Dating from the 1870s, it was again found through the family's connections: the grandfather of the current owner, Lord Rochdale, was a cotton merchant, like Beatrix's grandfather. Lingholm had fifteen bedrooms, and was set in its own parkland reaching down to the lake shores. Its east-facing aspect afforded great views across the lake but, as Beatrix complained, it was very exposed to the chill east wind coming over the mountains.

Beatrix's painting of the stairs at Lingholm shows the hall and high stairwell of the big, draughty house, and its abundance of Gothic Revival woodwork. 'It is a curious (& unpleasant) place for atmosphere, very stuffy . . .' she wrote. It was lit, until well into the 1890s when electric lighting was gradually coming in, by gas.

Opposite: Lingholm, photographed by Rupert Potter.

Above: The hall at Lingholm by Beatrix.

Outside the Lingholm sitting room, on a gentle summer's day, the Potters might take tea on the paved terrace and look over the garden to the strip of native woodland bordering the lake. In the early 1900s, many of the trees would have been maybe fifty years old, more slender, less tall and dense, and the view across the lake more open. Today, you can walk down to the lake shore as Beatrix must have done, winding through the beech trees to the narrow rocky shore. The formal gardens of today were developed in the early 1900s; on one side of the broad grassy terraces is a flagstoned court with a B-shaped pond, named after Beatrice, the wife of Colonel George Kemp, later Lord Rochdale.

The woodland, short-turfed fields and lake shore of Lingholm provided fertile territory for a range of fungi, which Beatrix painted with a naturalist's eye for detail. There are field mushrooms, *amanita* and *russula* species in the parkland around Lingholm today. The moist climate and characteristic mix of woodland, fell and fields have made the Lake District rich in fungi, including some European rarities.

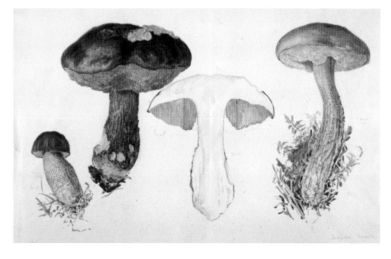

DERWENTWATER

Right: Beatrix's watercolour sketch of Derwentwater.

Below left: Squirrel Nutkin's singing and dancing are in keeping with the wild squirrel's natural character. They gesticulate with their bushy tails, and use them for balance. Just like Nutkin, they are given to tail flicking and foot stamping, and 'talk' a lot, by means of a variety of chattering, growling and moaning sounds.

Below right: The red squirrels 'made little rafts out of twigs, and they paddled away over the water to Owl Island to gather nuts.' This scene in *The Tale of Squirrel Nutkin* shows the view from the northwestern lake shore looking towards the wooded hump of St Herbert's island (called Owl Island in the story).

Maybe it was when Beatrix was strolling through beech woodland that she spotted 'a most comical little squirrel' which had lost most of its tail. 'It was so impertinent,' she wrote in a letter in 1901 to Norah Moore, one of her former governess's daughters. 'He chattered and clattered and threw down acorns on to my head . . . I believe that his name was Nutkin and that he had a brother called Twinkleberry.' That summer Beatrix was at Lingholm working on the backgrounds for the story that would become *The Tale of Squirrel Nutkin.*

The Lake District is one of the few areas of England where there are still populations of red squirrels like Nutkin. They are smaller than their invasive grey North American cousins, and have rather distinguished ear tufts when in their winter coats.

The principal setting for *The Tale of Squirrel Nutkin* is St Herbert's Island, one of the Derwentwater islets that are like temporarily anchored rafts of vegetation. It takes its name from a seventh-century hermit who lived on the island. In the Tale, however, the island resident is Old Brown the owl to whom the squirrels pay tribute. The islands have retained their native woodland, never having been grazed to destruction, though some have been planted with introduced species such as rhododendron.

Above: Nuts are the favourite food of red squirrels, particularly those from the Scots Pine – one squirrel can extract the thirty or so nuts per cone from as many as a hundred and fifty cones a day! Squirrels sharpen their teeth on bark, bones and stones, leaving visible scratch marks.

Fawe Park Latitude 54:35:36N Longitude 3:09:22 W Landranger map reference NY253226

Above: Fawe Park in its setting in 1897.

For one summer only, in 1903, the Potters rented Fawe Park, the neighbouring estate to Lingholm. Its setting, garden and details provided Beatrix with the backgrounds for *The Tale of Benjamin Bunny*, published in 1904. Benjamin was named after Benjamin Bouncer, the pet rabbit Beatrix had owned ten years previously, who had been the model for her first greetings cards and who had been taken along on many family holidays, travelling in a covered basket.

Fawe Park is privately owned, but you can see parts of the house and garden from the public right of way that runs from Silver Hill just above the lake shore to Derwent Bank.

Above left: A portrait of the real Benjamin Bunny.

Above right: Sketches of garden paraphernalia at Fawe Park were used as backgrounds for *The Tale of Benjamin Bunny*.

Left: Looking across Derwentwater towards the fells. The views over lake and fell are breathtaking, but in her sketches, as here, Beatrix often focused on the smaller picture, with a section of landscape that shows her appreciation of the rocks and how the land was formed.

Right: Looking over Derwentwater to Walla Crag rising up behind the soft, floating spinney of St Herbert's Island.

Opposite: A view over Ashness Bridge to the vale of Keswick.

Beatrix would have explored the eastern shores of Derwentwater in a pony and trap. Today you can drive along the same road, which follows a narrow, winding strip between lake and hillside.

About halfway along this road Walla Crag rises sheer and rugged to the east. If Beatrix took one of the clear paths leading to the crag, she would have seen lake and islands, the vale of Keswick and Bassenthwaite Lake spread beneath her. In the picture opposite the path to the right leads up towards the summit of Walla Crag, and in the opposite direction to Castlerigg Fell and High Seat.

Opposite: View from Cat Bells, looking west over the Newlands Valley with the sun about to set behind Causey Pike.

Left: Studies of Mrs Tiggy-winkle's head.

Above: The Newlands Valley from Beatrix's 1903 sketchbook. The same view appears as a background in *The Tale of Mrs. Tiggy-Winkle* (see page 59).

Below: Mrs Tiggy-winkle and Lucie set out to deliver the laundry in this illustration from the book.

'It really strikes me that some scenery is almost theatrical, or ultra-romantic,' Beatrix once wrote in her journal, a description that fits the view of the Newlands Valley from Cat Bells, seen opposite. Newlands Valley, to the west of Derwentwater, was an area Beatrix explored thoroughly. It is an enclosed world of its own, cut off from Derwentwater by the ridge of Cat Bells, and coming to an abrupt end at the buttresses of steep surrounding mountain slopes. It lies south of the Vale of Keswick and the Potter holiday lets of Lingholm and Fawe Park.

Newlands Valley was most famously the setting for *The Tale of Mrs. Tiggy-Winkle*, the hedgehog who ran a laundry service on the slopes of Cat Bells fell. Beatrix's pet hedgehog was the model. 'As long as she can go to sleep on my knee she is delighted, but if she is propped up on end for half an hour, she first begins to yawn pathetically, and then she does bite! Nevertheless she is a dear person.'

The gentle, pastoral landscape of the Newlands Valley floor reaches like a tongue into the surrounding fells. Beatrix explored the narrow, tumbling lanes that link farms and hamlets on either side of the vale in her pony and trap, and the sketches she made became the setting for *The Tale of Mrs. Tiggy-Winkle*. A lane runs a circular route up one side of the valley and back down the other – for the valley is a dead-end – clinging to the lower slopes of the fells, and dipping to elbow over a narrow stone bridge at the valley head.

Opposite: Newlands Valley in autumn.

Above left: Looking north over the Newlands Valley towards Derwentwater.

Above right: Little Town, the hamlet in the centre of the Newlands Valley, is transformed in *The Tale of Mrs. Tiggy-Winkle* into a farm called Little-town, Lucie's home.

Left: Lucie runs along the steep path above the valley in *The Tale of Mrs. Tiggy-Winkle*. The path she took was an old track to the mines.

DERWENTWATER

Above left: Mrs Tiggy-winkle's front door, leading 'straight into the hill', looks like the entrance to an old mine.

Left: Beatrix's 1899 sketch of a similar mine entrance near Grasmere.

Above: The summit of Cat Bells.

Opposite: The view of the Newlands Valley from Cat Bells. The lake in the distance is Bassenthwaite.

The spine of Cat Bells (opposite) forms the eastern wall of the Newlands Valley, and it is on its lower slopes that Mrs Tiggy-winkle lived. You can follow in the steps of Lucie as she searched for her pocket handkerchiefs, but you will see a softer landscape than she, or Beatrix Potter, saw. A film of wiry moorland grass covers some of the spoil heaps and the cobbled smelting sites of the old mine workings. In the early 1900s the lead mines were practically worked out although there was some small-scale activity, but the scars they left behind were still fresh.

Cat Bells Altitude 451 m Latitude 54:34:05N Longitude 3:10:14W Landranger map reference NY244198

To the west and north of Derwentwater there is some magnificent scenery and the Potters certainly did some sightseeing in this area, although travelling farther afield was a major undertaking. Beatrix reported a family trip by horse-drawn carriage in 1885: 'Went to Buttermere by Grange, Honister and back by Newlands. Extraordinary and striking drive, but one to make one thankful to see a field of corn; an awful road. Never knew what jolting was before, three of the party including self, excessively ill following night; recommend said excursion as a cure for colic.'

The party would nevertheless have seen some beautiful views from their carriage during this trip.

DERWENTWATER

Right: A winter view of Grange-in-Borrowdale. When the Potter family made their trip to Buttermere, they travelled via Grange.

Opposite: Looking towards Derwentwater from Grange Crags.

Skiddaw Height 931 m Latitude 54:38:53N Longitude 3:08:47W Landranger map reference NY261287

Looking north from Derwentwater, the views are dominated by Skiddaw, one of the Lake District's highest peaks. The steep, barren slopes of Skiddaw (pronounced 'Skidder' locally) erupt from a gentler, civilized landscape of parkland planted with specimen trees, probably by a Lancashire landowner. The mountain has given its name to the dark Skiddaw slates, the most ancient rocks in the Lake District, that form its rounded outline.

Opposite, above and left: The view of the snow-dusted summit of Skiddaw across Derwentwater varies endlessly according to the time of day and the light.

SETTLING IN SAWREY

Settling in Sawrey

Previous page: Hill Top Farm, at Near Sawrey, was bought by Beatrix in 1905. 'I prefer a pastoral landscape backed by mountains,' she wrote in her journal; the countryside around the village of Sawrey fitted the bill. Hill Top is set among a lumpy counterpane of fields and copses, with Coniston fell rising in the background like a separate, distant world.

Above: Beatrix's 1905 sketch of Hill Top Farm, as it was when she first bought it.

Opposite: The view from the garden at Hill Top.

A cluster of farm buildings, traditional Lake District cottages and orchards nestle among fields on the edge of a charming village; a cameo of perfect countryside where time seems to have stood still. This is Near Sawrey, where thirty-nine-year-old Beatrix bought a property as soon as she was able to do so, with independent income from her book sales and a legacy from an aunt. It is where she eventually lived, married and belonged, and where she lives on still, in the places immortalized in her books, and in her contribution to the countryside and its traditional lifestyle.

A turning point came in Beatrix's life in 1905. Although Beatrix was by now just short of forty, she was still expected to carry out the duties of an unmarried daughter in keeping with Victorian middle-class values. She was tied to her parents' London household and obliged to go on the family holidays. But then she received a proposal of marriage from her publisher, Norman Warne, with whom she had been working closely throughout the production of all her books. Marriage to Norman offered new happiness and the prospect of freedom. However tragically her fiancé contracted a virulent form of leukaemia and died just a month after their engagement. It seemed the devastating end of her hopes for a new life. But it was also to prove the beginning of a permanent and deepening relationship with the Lake District. Though her dreams had been shattered, Beatrix dealt with her grief by immersing herself in one of her most productive periods as author and illustrator . . . and into the farm she had just bought in Sawrey. The purchase of Hill Top Farm was her first independent and permanent commitment to the Lake District. She escaped there as often as she could, though back in her role as unmarried daughter, she was barely able to spend a month there in the year following her purchase. Nevertheless, little by little, she became increasingly absorbed in the community and the country way of life.

Above: The cat family go up the path to their home in *The Tale of Tom Kitten*.

Opposite: The path leading to the front porch at Hill Top today.

Sawrey actually encompasses two villages, named Far Sawrey and Near Sawrey according to their distance from Hawkshead. Hill Top Farm is located in Near Sawrey, a hamlet that was picture-book pretty even before Beatrix preserved it forever in her tales. The rooms you see at Hill Top today are those that Samuel and Anna Maria Whiskers raided; the farmyards, lanes and gardens of Sawrey are where Jemima Puddle-duck and Tom Kitten walked. It is the heart of Beatrix Potter's world, and, bar the tourist traffic, is so little changed that to visit is like walking into the pages of the tales.

In the frontispiece picture of *The Tale of the Pie and The Patty-Pan* published 1905 (see next page), Hill Top farmhouse is lime-washed white as it was when Beatrix bought it. Today, the render that covers the slate-built house is left plain, the paintwork green. The oldest parts of the house are seventeenth-century; the sash windows were installed in the 1800s.

Above: Mrs Cannon was the tenant farmer's wife at Hill Top; she and her children, Ralph and Betsy, feature in *The Tale of Jemima Puddle-duck*.

Right: The frontispiece picture from *The Tale of The Pie and The Patty-Pan*, with Hill Top in the background.

John Cannon was the tenant farmer at Hill Top when Beatrix bought it. She was impressed by the way in which he ran the farm, and asked him to stay on. She designed and had built a new wing for the Cannon family to live in, in keeping with local vernacular architecture. Beatrix and her visitors stayed in the main part of the original house.

Several years later, Beatrix became further entrenched in the area when she married local solicitor, William Heelis. They lived in a second property Beatrix had bought in 1909, Castle Farm. But Beatrix continued to use Hill Top as an office, for entertaining visitors and fans, and most significantly, as her 'treasure house'. Each room was a set piece that she carefully arranged, and so it remains today, as she requested in her will.

Hill Top Latitude 54:21:02N Longitude 2:58:14W Landranger map reference SD370954

Above: Typically a cluster of Lakeland farm buildings, such as those at Hill Top, housed a byre for pigs and cattle, storage places for grain and animal fodder, farm tools and equipment, a cart, and a threshing floor.

Left: Beatrix's sketch for a new wing for the Cannons to live in at Hill Top. Beatrix continued to use the main (right-hand) part of the original house. The 'new' wing can be seen far left, and is just visible in the photograph above, to the right of the farm buildings.

Opposite: Looking through the window at Hill Top.

Above: The view from the roof is recreated in *The Tale of Samuel Whiskers*, with Stoney Lane winding up and over the hill.

Below: Tom Kitten contemplates escaping up the chimney over the kitchen range, in *The Tale of Samuel Whiskers*.

The main room at Hill Top, as in every traditional Lake District farmhouse, was the 'fireroom', which served as kitchen, dining room, and hall, and from which stairs and other rooms in the house lead. The kitchen range – and this one at Hill Top, which features in the tales of *Samuel Whiskers* and *The Pie and The Patty-Pan*, must be the best known in the world – was the heart of the home, originally the only source of heat, and where all the cooking was done. Beatrix collected old oak furniture, like the Georgian dresser, chairs and gate-leg table with turned uprights, all found at local sales and farm auctions.

Above: The 'pretty dresser, with crooked legs' that Beatrix bought for the hall at Hill Top. Anna Maria speeds past the same dresser in *The Tale of Samuel Whiskers*.

Above right: The room known as the 'New Room'.

Opposite: The parlour at Hill Top.

Originally, the parlour in a traditional Lake District house doubled as a bedroom, but Beatrix upgraded the one at Hill Top, installing an Adam-style fireplace and elegant mahogany furniture. She was an avid collector of ornaments and curios. Some are displayed in the parlour, others are in what Beatrix called her 'Treasure Room'. In the photograph opposite a selection of the silhouettes beloved by the Victorians hang on the wall beside the fireplace and two Wedgwood floral plates are suspended above the mantel shelf.

The room pictured above was known as the New Room, and it was where Beatrix sat to write. It housed an oak bureau bookcase and some of her brother Bertram's big oil paintings. The 1730 walnut bureau and Chippendale-style chairs that can be seen in this photograph were moved from another of Beatrix's farms, Troutbeck Park Farm, after her death, in keeping with the request in her will that 'any other objects of interest belonging to me in any other of my cottages and farmhouses' should be preserved at Hill Top.

Right: The staircase and half-landing at Hill Top with Beatrix's long-case clock.

Above: Mrs Tabitha Twitchit passes the same clock as she searches for her son Tom in *The Tale of Samuel Whiskers*.

Below: A mouse-hole under a Hill Top door, evidence of former resident mice.

Opposite: The top of the staircase where Samuel Whiskers appears with his rolling-pin.

'Mrs Tabitha went up and down all over the house, mewing for Tom Kitten . . . It was an old, old house, full of cupboards and passages. Some of the walls were four feet thick, and there used to be queer noises inside them, as if there might be a little secret staircase.' (*The Tale of Samuel Whiskers*). In addition to having an intriguing layout, Hill Top is an antique collector's paradise, for Beatrix loved old furniture with burnished wood and classical lines, like the eighteenth-century walnut-veneered long-case clock on the staircase (shown opposite).

When Samuel Whiskers steals a rolling-pin from the farmhouse kitchen in *The Tale of Samuel Whiskers* he runs up the very staircase you can see at Hill Top today. The real rats that visited Hill Top Farm were discouraged, however. When Mrs Cannon saw a rat 'sitting up eating its dinner under the kitchen table in the middle of the afternoon', several cats were brought in, zinc strips put along the bottom of the doors and the skirting boards cemented.

Right: The limestone fireplace with carved wood mantel in Beatrix's bedroom.

Below: Detail of Beatrix's embroidery for the bed valance.

Opposite: Overall view of the bedroom.

Beatrix bought the seventeenth-century four-poster bed, in the upstairs bedroom at Hill Top, from a local farm. The tester (the 'roof') above the bed protects the sleepers from dust and insects. Beatrix started embroidering the green cotton damask valance in 1935, working with old-gold-coloured silk, and finished it four years later when she was in her seventy-third year. The wallpaper in the bedroom is William Morris's 'Daisy' pattern which Beatrix chose herself. 'For a background to my four-poster nothing could be better, except tapestry.'

Above: This cabinet of ruby glass and Oriental and European porcelain was among the items that were transferred to Hill Top from Beatrix's study at Troutbeck Park Farm.

Below: Section of a showcase displaying mementos, including a set of miniature bronze figures of the characters from Beatrix's books.

BEATRIX POTTER'S **LAKE DISTRICT**

Beatrix was interested in collecting china and ornamental items and enjoyed arranging them decoratively in cabinets. Most of her collections are displayed in the 'Treasure Room', and include many objects which she requested should be moved to Hill Top from her other properties after her death. Also on display in this room is a doll's house which contains the original dishes of plaster food that Hunca Munca and Tom Thumb stole in *The Tale of Two Bad Mice*.

Above: A shelf on top of the Hill Top doll's house is filled with shells, miniature fans and other dolls' accessories. The central feature is Peter Rabbit's famous red and white spotted handkerchief from *The Tale of Benjamin Bunny*.

Left: The front of the doll's house.

Opposite: A cabinet containing carved ivory pieces such as chessmen, Japanese netsuke figures and original quill boxes.

As well as renovating the interior of Hill Top, Beatrix concerned herself with improving the surroundings of her new home. While the Cannons concentrated on running the farm, she threw herself into transforming the garden. She had paths and sculptural features made from locally quarried stone, and mixed the pretty with the practical, planting flowers such as antirrhinums and roses among vegetables and beneath fruit trees.

'I am being inundated with offers of plants!' she wrote. There were 'splendid phloxes' from a local quarryman, a newspaper bundle of saxifrage from Mrs Taylor at the corner cottage, honesty that had been 'put out to be burnt in a heap of garden refuse'. She bought lilac, rhododendron, red fuchsia ('they say it will grow out of doors here all winter') from a Windermere nursery,

and paid two shillings and sixpence (about 12p) for an azalea plant. Taking a tip from the blacksmith's wife, Mrs Satterthwaite, who told her that 'stolen plants always grow', Beatrix 'impudently took a large basket and trowel with me . . . I got nice things in handfuls without any shame, amongst others a bundle of lavender slips.'

The National Trust gardener has reconstructed the Hill Top gardens in keeping with Beatrix's own ideas, with traditional cottage-garden plants such as roses, feverfew, geraniums, hollyhocks, honeysuckle, lupins and snapdragons. He could find clues to her taste in books such as *The Tale of The Pie and The Patty-Pan* and *The Tale of Tom Kitten*, although he chuckled, 'Mrs Heelis sometimes used a bit of illustrator's licence. The flowers don't always bloom together as they do in her pictures.'

Opposite: The garden at Hill Top, a mixture of flowers and vegetables.

Above: Illustrations from *The Tale of The Pie and The Patty-Pan* (left) and *The Tale of Tom Kitten* (right) demonstrate Beatrix's delight in flowers.

Above: The vegetable garden in spring.

Opposite above: The beehive inside the bee-bole.

Opposite below: Beatrix arranged the construction of new paths from locally quarried stone.

When Beatrix first moved to Hill Top the only garden was a small square area opposite the front door. She kept this walled space as a kitchen garden. In the wall is a 'bee-bole', a recess for sheltering bee skeps, which Beatrix made use of. 'I found a swarm of bees on Sunday and caught them (it isn't quite so valiant as it sounds!) . . . We think they had been blown out of a tree; they were very numbed but they are all right now and a fine swarm. No one in the village has lost them and I don't mean to inquire further afield!'

SETTLING IN SAWREY

The orchard at Hill Top already had a few old cooking apple trees, to which Beatrix added new young trees, including pears and plums. In the uncut grass of the orchard in early spring, clusters of snowdrops bloomed first, then came delicate-flowered wild daffodils, known locally as Lent lilies, and, with the warmth and first showers the trees themselves burst into blossom. Beatrix even cultivated a grape vine against the warm brick walls: 'I have got three bunches [of grapes] . . . but I doubt if they will ever ripen out of doors.'

'I like old walls,' Beatrix commented in a letter to Norman Warne's sister, Millie, in 1906. The fern in the wall on which Tom, Moppet and Mittens sit in *The Tale of Tom Kitten* (opposite) may have been planted by Beatrix herself, salvaged from an old stone bridge by Esthwaite Water. The kittens look into the lane, where, in the early 1900s, horse-drawn traffic was still the norm; Beatrix was 'entitled to all the road sweepings' [of manure] along the section that bordered her property.

Left: The garden at Hill Top is a profusion of flowers, trees, vegetables and herbs.

Above: Many unusual flowers flourish in the damp, cool weather of the Lake District. Astrantia, Sea Holly and Thalictrum (above from top) can be found at Hill Top.

Above left: Near Sawrey photographed by Rupert Potter.

Above right: Near Sawrey village under a sprinkling of snow.

Right: The village pub, the Tower Bank Arms, today and as it appears in *The Tale of Jemima Puddle-Duck*.

Hill Top is located just off the road that runs through the village of Near Sawrey. The road is recognizable from the photograph, above left, that Beatrix's father Rupert took in 1913. But the village has a more spruced-up air today, in keeping with its status as a tourist attraction and shrine to its most famous inhabitant.

The village pub, the Tower Bank Arms was – and is – just on the other side of the Hill Top garden wall. Beatrix doesn't mention being a customer there but she may, as she confessed to doing after agricultural shows, have sometimes sat among her fellow farmers and villagers to discuss local affairs.

Opposite: Buckle Yeat Cottage, now a guest house.

Above left: Beatrix reworked this watercolour painting of the front garden at Buckle Yeat for an illustration for *The Tale of The Pie and The Patty-Pan* (below).

Above right: The Jemima Puddle-duck weather vane on the roof of Buckle Yeat.

Beatrix used many real Sawrey locations and characters in her books. Duchess's front garden in *The Tale of The Pie and The Patty-Pan* can be identified even today by its gateposts and wall of upright slabs of local stone as Buckle Yeat Cottage. Duchess was modelled on the pedigree Pomeranian owned by Mrs Rogerson who later became Beatrix and William's housekeeper. Ribby, the cat who asked Duchess to tea, was probably one of the Hill Top cats, but in the book, she lives in one of the three Lakefield cottages at the edge of the village, which Beatrix had visited when she was on holiday with her family in 1896 and 1902.

Above: This cottage, Meadowcroft, previously housed the village shop which features in *The Tale of Ginger and Pickles* (top).

Right: Beatrix sketched the inside of the shop as a background for the story.

Opposite: The crossroads behind Hill Top, the spot from which Pigling and Alexander began their journey in *The Tale of Pigling Bland*.

The village corner shop in Near Sawrey was the setting for *The Tale of Ginger and Pickles.* It was owned by John Taylor in Beatrix's day, and she dedicated the book to him. When it was published in 1909, Beatrix wrote to Norman Warne's sister, Millie, 'It has got a good many views which can be recognized in the village . . . they are all quite jealous of each others' houses and cats getting into a book.'

On the outskirts of Sawrey, just behind Hill Top Farm, is the intersection of village lanes that formed the setting for the frontispiece of *The Tale of Pigling Bland*. Other inspiration came from the farm: 'I spent a very wet hour inside the pig stye drawing the pig. It tries to nibble my boots, which is interrupting.'

Above: Beatrix and her mother outside Castle Farm before the extension was built.

Opposite: Castle Farm today.

Below: Rupert Potter photographed Beatrix and William on the eve of their wedding in October 1913.

Beatrix bought Castle Farm across the fields from Hill Top in 1909, joining up the lands of the two farms into a single, more manageable unit.

The Hawkshead solicitor who advised her on buying her land and property was William Heelis. In 1913 Beatrix and William married. They moved together into the late eighteenth-century Castle Cottage, the farmhouse of Castle Farm, where Beatrix was to live until her death forty years later. She was free at last from the duty of looking after her parents' home and able to embark on another stage in her Lake District immersion.

Beatrix and Wiliam extended Castle Cottage, more than doubling its size. In 1924, she described the garden to a young friend: 'I have lots of flowers . . . It is a regular old fashioned farm garden, with a box hedge round the flower bed, and moss roses and pansies and blackcurrants and strawberries and peas – and big sage bushes for Jemima, but onions always do badly. I have tall white bell flowers I am fond of . . . next there will be phlox; and last come the michaelmas daisies and chrysanthemums.'

From the lane above Post Office Meadow, you can see Castle Cottage to best effect, with the sweep of stone-walled field before it, and the hills that rise to Moss Eccles Tarn behind. To walk to her first farm, Beatrix would leave Castle Cottage by the garden gate, cross the farm lane and then the meadow, at the top of which was the main road through the village and the entrance to Hill Top.

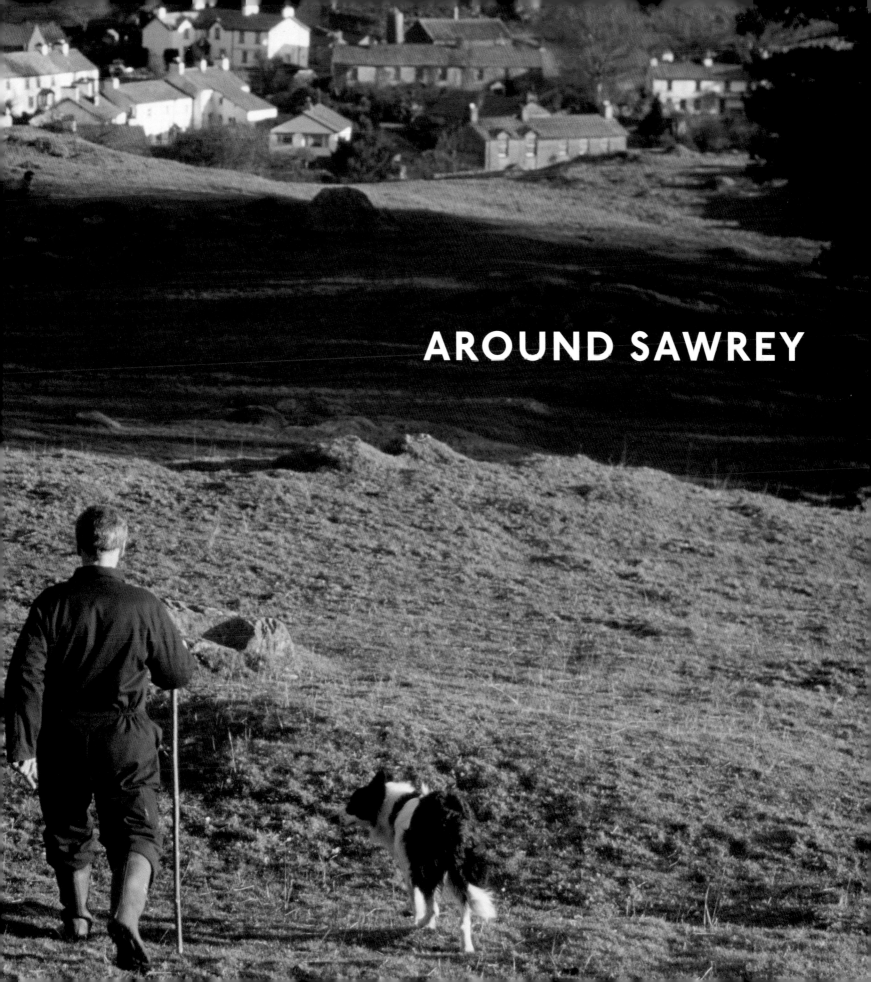

AROUND SAWREY

Around Sawrey

As the number of Beatrix's little books increased, she, like Jemima Puddle-duck, began to spread her wings, moving her tales away from the farmyards, streets and houses of the village into the countryside beyond.

Around the village, crazy-shaped small fields of grey-green turf tumble over the land, delineated by stone walls (they say that the size of a field is dictated by how far you can throw a stone to make the boundary wall) and softened by russet clumps of marsh grass, a brush of coppiced woodland or tuft of spinney. The vastness of Lake Windermere is just over the hill, but you would not know it was there, so contained is this bowl of gentle countryside rimmed by the fells.

This is the countryside that Beatrix came to know best. She walked the ancient farm paths, through the foothills and up to the highland tarns and barren hilltops, from where waves of fells roll into the far distance, and lakes lie like gems in the valleys far below. From here you see the windblown weather race over the fells, and, split up by the hills, cast sunshine on one little valley and spill rain on the next. As Beatrix explored, observed and learned the pattern of country life through the year, she got to know the people who lived there and became involved in their lives.

The motor car brought a new wave of independent tourists to the Lake District. In October 1929, Beatrix reported: 'We went through the Tarns roads where we met about fifteen cars and no room to pass.' Today, there are many times more tourists and cars, but the country lanes remain as they have always been, squeezed into the available space between lake and fell or straining up an uncompromising hill, with no room to pass, or to stop and look or walk.

Above: Jemima Puddle-duck flies away from the farm and the countryside opens out beneath her.

Opposite: Jemima would have seen this view of Esthwaite Water, with Langdale Pikes in the distance.

Previous spread: A modern-day shepherd returns to the village of Sawrey, enfolded by the swell and dip and turn of the landscape in which it sits.

The road from Sawrey to Hawkshead passes above Esthwaite Water. When Jemima Puddle-duck left the farm in search of a safe place to lay her eggs, she flew over the waters of Esthwaite and its surrounding hills and fields. The views in *The Tale of Mr. Jeremy Fisher*, published a year after Beatrix bought Hill Top Farm, are also of Esthwaite Water. The photograph opposite highlights the contrast that Beatrix saw between her 'green and pleasant' lowlands around Sawrey and the high fells of Langdale Pikes, like the stage set of an opera.

Opposite: Esthwaite Water.

Above: Beatrix painted several landscapes of the lake in its valley setting, including this one at harvest-time.

Below: Mr Jeremy Fisher goes boating against a backdrop of Esthwaite Water.

Right: Fishing on Esthwaite Water today. Beatrix, her father and her husband William all enjoyed fishing.

Moss Eccles Latitude 54:21 :43N Longitude 2:58: 10W Landranger map reference SD371967

One of Beatrix and William's favourite spots for fishing was Moss Eccles Tarn, high above Esthwaite Water. The still waters of Moss Eccles fill a natural depression fed by water-catchment from the rolling contours of its setting. It is framed today by small plantations of spruce and larch, introduced since Beatrix's time, and healthy groups of native wetland trees such as alder and willow.

Beatrix and William used to walk up to Moss Eccles Tarn. A heavy boat, double-bowed so that you could row in either direction and flat-bottomed for the shallow waters, would be hauled from the old boathouse, and William would fish for trout or perch while Beatrix painted. A local bailiff recalled how Mrs Heelis would be dressed in a shapeless, coarse wool suit spun from the wool of her own Herdwick sheep. There would be no fancy picnic; just a tin box with cheese sandwiches. Beatrix introduced the red and white waterlilies, which can still be seen today.

The original boat Beatrix and William used is on display at the Windermere Steamboat Museum in Bowness.

Above: Beatrix Potter's characters look perfectly natural among the alleys and quaint buildings of Hawkshead, as in this picture from *The Tale of The Pie and The Patty-Pan*.

Below: Johnny Town-mouse with his briefcase and bag of golf clubs.

Opposite: William Heelis's solicitors' office, now the Beatrix Potter Gallery housing a collection of her original art.

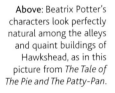

Just as in the old days when the Potters holidayed at Wray Castle, Hawkshead was still Beatrix's nearest market town when she lived in Sawrey. Hawkshead has two main streets and three squares, and terraces of quaint lime-washed houses with upper floors overhanging alleys and courtyards.

W H Heelis & Sons, the solicitors' office where Beatrix's husband William worked, was left to the National Trust on his death. It is next door to the aptly named Bend-or-Bump Cottage. It is said that the cover illustration of *The Tale of Johnny Town-Mouse* is modelled on the Hawkshead doctor with whom William Heelis played golf. Many of the locals have 'Mrs Heelis' stories to tell, and one of them is that Willie would pretend to be hard at work in his office when Beatrix came into town, but as soon as she drove off, he would nip out with his friend the doctor for an afternoon's golf.

Grasmere Latitude 54:27:25N Longitude 3:01:40W Landranger map reference NY334073

Ambleside, seven miles away from Sawrey, was Beatrix's nearest post town. She could catch a ferry from the pier near Sawrey to Waterhead, at the head of Lake Windermere. Beatrix was a supporter of the Armitt Library in Ambleside, a subscription library with a valuable collection of scientific, literary and antiquarian material. She left a large number of her fungus pictures to the Armitt Trust on her death, and the paintings are now housed in the Armitt Museum in Ambleside.

The area north of Ambleside was already famous in Beatrix's day for its local beauty spots such as Grasmere. The pretty village, known for its prestigious inhabitants such as William and Dorothy Wordsworth, Samuel Taylor Coleridge and Thomas de Quincey, had become an essential part of the British 'Grand Tour'.

Above and left: Grasmere. The trees and surrounding hills are perfectly reflected in the still water.

Opposite below: *Lepiota friesii* which Beatrix found on a rubbish heap at Wray Castle in September 1894. The painting is now in the Armitt Musuem, Ambleside.

Above: Tarn Hows
under a stormy sky.

The road west out of Ambleside goes to the town of Coniston, passing another much-visited beauty spot, Tarn Hows.

'Tarn Hows is too theatrical for my taste; like scene painting,' commented Beatrix. To stand at any of the many viewpoints above the Tarn is to be overwhelmed by a complexity of shapes, folds and distances, multiple perspectives of mountain rims and, on a fine day, the intensity of colours.

Left: Beatrix painted Coniston Moor in November 1909. 'The colours are most lovely in the sunshine, all the leaves are off the trees, but the copse wood and fern on the hills keep their colour all winter.'

Opposite: A view of Coniston Water.

Below: The steam gondola on Coniston Water.

The area around Coniston Water is one of the oldest settled parts of the Lake District. The lake is not one of the most dramatically imposing but it has a quiet understated beauty. 'It is so compact and the ground and vegetation so varied,' Beatrix wrote.

The sheltered aspect of the lake means that it has always been a popular venue for various kinds of boating. A luxurious steam yacht gondola was launched on Coniston in 1859. Now fully restored by the National Trust, it still makes circuits of the lake today.

Opposite and below:
Views of the slate quarry at Tilberthwaite.

Left: During the family holidays Beatrix had fearlessly explored the local quarries looking for fossils. She identified them at the Natural History Museum close to her London home, and made detailed drawings.

North of Coniston, Tilberthwaite quarries slash through the land that rises from the hidden vale of Tilberthwaite on the Monk Coniston Estate that Beatrix bought in 1929. Today, the quarries are deep, dangerous gashes in the rock, no longer worked for the slate that provided the high quality building and roofing material for traditional houses. Nearby, a terrace of cottages, strangely isolated from the homely valley floor, are the abandoned homes of the former quarryworkers.

BEATRIX POTTER'S **LAKE DISTRICT**

Left: The Langdale Valley.

Above: Sunset over Langdale Pikes with Elterwater in the foreground.

Beatrix wrote of 'the sublime beauty of the silent lonely hills' that lay beyond her sheltered world of Sawrey. A few miles north, the Langdale Pikes erupt from the head of Great Langdale, a text-book example of a U-shaped glaciated valley with its flat, broad-bottomed floor and precipitous rocky side walls. The great tongue of the valley, with its undersized beck, meanders down to Elterwater, which in turn drains via the Brathay Valley into the north-west corner of Windermere near Ambleside.

Above: Great Langdale.

Right: Pig-wig dances with joy at the sight of the open hills in *The Tale of Pigling Bland*.

Opposite above: Looking west across the River Brathay.

Opposite below: Pigling Bland and Pig-wig escape over Brathay Bridge.

The Brathay river runs from Elterwater, at the meeting point of the Little and Great Langdale valleys, into the north-west tip of Lake Windermere. Beatrix thought this area, with its dip and rise of small fields and spinneys, 'very pretty'. In *The Tale of Pigling Bland* the two young pigs, on the run from the farmer who wants to make them into bacon, watched as 'the sunshine crept down the slopes into the peaceful green valleys, where little white cottages nestled in gardens and orchards.' They ran down from the hills and crossed the Brathay river, hand in hand, to make their escape over the hills and far away.

GETTING INVOLVED

Getting involved

Previous spread: Troutbeck Park Farm lies where the Troutbeck Valley ends and the high fells begin, 'a place of silence and whispering echoes. It is a mighty table-land between two streams,' Beatrix wrote. Her purchase of the Troutbeck Park Estate in 1924 established her as an active and involved landowner, and was an important focus for her conservation activities.

Opposite: Little Langdale. Valleys such as this were vulnerable targets for developers wanting to build holiday homes and other tourist facilities, but Beatrix bought much of the land, together with traditional farms and buildings, and ensured their conservation by leaving them to the National Trust.

'There are several rows going on [in the village]. But I am not in any of them at present – though much inclined!' Beatrix wrote in 1906, a year after she had bought Hill Top. She had rapidly become part of village life, even though she still had to split her time between London and Sawrey. Over the next few years, letters to her friends included many a comment on the state of crops, the weather, the price of butter or the demand for mutton, as she began to take an active part in running Hill Top and Castle farms. Little by little, Beatrix Potter, illustrator and storyteller, faded into the background, and with her marriage in 1913, Mrs Heelis, farmer and countrywoman came to the fore. 'You wouldn't think she had it in her to do those beautiful things [the books],' Louisa Rhodes, cook to Beatrix's mother, Helen, said of Beatrix in her later years. 'All we associated her with were . . . her Wellingtons, ragged clothes – and sheep, . . . a mackintosh too big for her and a sort of soft, floppy hat.' And Beatrix herself mused late in life, that writing the little books seemed 'a long time ago; and in another world'.

With her outsider's perspective, Beatrix saw that local farming methods, buildings, and the unique Lake District countryside were threatened and began to take action to protect then. She fought on behalf of local farmers against rises in land tax and joined the local footpath association. In 1911, she campaigned to ban hydroplanes from Lake Windermere – the 'beastly fly-swimming spluttering aeroplane . . . that makes a noise like ten million bluebottles' – and a plane factory on the lake shore. One wonders what she would do about the Jaguar fighter jets that rip through the valleys today.

Most importantly for the Lake District and Britain's countryside heritage, income from her books and merchandise, such as colouring books, pottery and wallpaper, gave Beatrix the means to buy traditional buildings, farms and land with a view to conserving them for the future. She worked with the National Trust and was to be one of its most important early benefactors. Her ultimate act of involvement was to bequeath all her land and property to the National Trust.

Above: A Muscovy duck from Yew Tree Farm, one of Beatrix's properties.

Above right: 'I am much amused with six little ducks waddling about the garden,' Beatrix Potter wrote in 1913. 'They rush for presents of worms and caterpillars.'

Right: Pigling Bland spends the night in Mr Piperson's crowded hen house in *The Tale of Pigling Bland*.

Opposite: Free-range Speckled and Black Rock hens.

One of Beatrix's first steps to becoming a farmer, when she started to spend more time at Hill Top, was to look after the poultry – chickens, ducks and turkeys. Letters to her friends began to be filled with tales of farming life: 'I have got some white pullets . . . they are such pets, they will all try to jump on my knee at once if I sit on the doorstep, and two or three will allow me to pick them up and stroke them like a parrot. Their feet are rather dirty.' In 1912, she was invited to judge the trussed poultry at a local show.

Beatrix observed the characteristics of the farm animals and used them in stories such as *The Tale of Jemima Puddle-Duck*: Jemima has a reputation for being a 'bad sitter' and her eggs are taken away by the farmer's wife to be hatched by a broody hen.

John Cannon, the farm manager at Hill Top, organized a sale of the Hill Top pig stock shortly after Beatrix bought the farm. 'The whole district is planted out with my pigs . . . if they grow well, we shall "get a name for pigs". Such is fame!' Beatrix always retained a fondness for pigs. Her heroine in *The Tale of Pigling Bland* is a 'perfectly lovely little black Berkshire pig' with 'twinkly little screwed up eyes, a double chin, and a short turned up nose.'

Beatrix put a drawing of herself in *The Tale of Pigling Bland*, published in 1913 just before the First World War. During the war, many male farmworkers enlisted and Beatrix's work on the farm – now an amalgamation of Castle and Hill Top farms – was intensified. There were cattle and a hundred and twenty sheep, fodder crops to be sown, harvested and stored, bracken from the fells to be collected for winter bedding. Beatrix looked after the poultry, rabbits ('I'm afraid we do have rabbit pies of the young ones'), Dolly the pony and pet pig Sally, and she tended the garden.

Opposite: A black Berkshire piglet.

Above: Aunt Pettitoes looks after her large and unruly family in *The Tale of Pigling Bland* with some help from Miss Potter.

Above: Prize cups and certificates which Beatrix won for her sheep at local shows, on display at the Beatrix Potter Gallery.

Right: Beatrix and her shepherd Tom Storey pose beside a prize-winning sheep.

Left: Beatrix and her sheepdog Kep in the garden at Hill Top in 1913.

Below left: A painting of Kep on the wintry fells.

Below: Sketch of a cow sitting on grass. In 1907 there were six cows at Hill Top, named White Stockings, Garnett, Rose, Norah, Blossom and Kitchen, who was the best at giving milk. By 1910 Hill Top butter was being 'commended' at a local dairy show.

"Kep"
March 6.1909
Beatrix Potter

The cups on display at the Beatrix Potter Gallery in Hawkshead bear witness to Beatrix's success in managing her farms. She was passionate about the local Herdwick sheep, the only breed hardy enough to survive winter on the fells. Under the guidance of shepherd Tom Storey, Herdwick ewes from her farms won all the prizes at Keswick, Ennerdale, Eskdale, Loweswater and other local shows over eight consecutive years from 1930. 'You would laugh to see me, amongst the other old farmers (usually in a tavern!) after a sheep fair,' she wrote.

Over the years Beatrix got to know many a sheepdog and had her favourites such as Kep who features in *The Tale of Jemima Puddle-Duck*. As she grew more experienced, she knew the essential qualities of a good working dog, such as having a 'good nose' for finding sheep in the snow.

Beatrix was interested in the local architecture, both within Sawrey and in the country round about. She cared about the traditional features and furniture as well as the buildings themselves. She also understood the value of preserving the local community, which required a healthy, living cross-section of farmers, shopkeepers, and skilled workmen such as plumbers, carpenters and joiners.

As Beatrix began to expand her property holdings she bought many individual buildings, including shops and houses in Sawrey.

Opposite: Bird How Cottage, now a holiday home in Eskdale, is a well-preserved vernacular building of pink Eskdale granite and local slate.

Above: Townend in the Troutbeck Valley has a wealth of original features inside and out. Here you can see the slate ledge 'drip catcher' above the windows.

BEATRIX POTTER'S **LAKE DISTRICT**

Opposite: Townend Farm in the Troutbeck Valley.

Above: Troutbeck Park Farm which Beatrix bought in 1924.

Left: Troutbeck Park Farm was the setting for scenes in *The Fairy Caravan*, a book Beatrix wrote for her American market in 1929. The book is a medley of adventures, fairy tales and cameos of country life. Beatrix felt that Americans appreciated 'the memories of old times, the simple country pleasures' more than British readers.

Townend (opposite) stands at the entrance of a broad ice-carved valley that reaches deep into the high barren fells below Kirkstone Pass, north-east of Windermere. Beyond it is the 1,900-acre Troutbeck Park Estate that Beatrix Heelis bought in 1924. The Troutbeck Park land and farms were run down, the Herdwick sheep stock in poor condition. But in buying the land, Beatrix saved the valley from unsympathetic development. She also hired the shepherd from Townend Farm, Tom Storey, who was an expert in the breeding of Herdwicks, and together they built up an award-winning flock at Troutbeck Park.

'Mr Heelis and I are going to Coniston. There is a lovely stretch of mountain and valley to sell there . . . I am very interested because my great-grandfather had land there and I have always longed to buy it back and give it to the Trust in remembrance.' Beatrix wrote this to a young American friend, Henry P. Coolidge, in October 1929. Her grandfather, Abraham Crompton (1757–1829), a Lancashire cotton merchant, bought Holme Ground Farm in 1810. After his death it was sold on, and came up for sale again in 1929, when Beatrix was 64. It was part of a parcel of some 4,000 acres of land and seven farms known as the Monk Coniston Estate, lying between the valley of Little Langdale, north of Lake Windermere, and Coniston Water. Beatrix bought the estate with money earned from her American book sales, saving the land from being sold for afforestation. She subsequently sold half of the land to the National Trust once they had raised sufficient funds. By now an astute businesswoman, she 'got back three-quarters of the original purchase money of Monk Coniston . . . and kept the more valuable half of the estate.' On her death, however, the balance of the estate was left to the Trust.

BEATRIX POTTER'S **LAKE DISTRICT**

Beatrix described the Monk Coniston Estate as 'an enormous scattered piece'. At the northern end the farms in the Little Langdale area have spectacular settings.

Just above Low Hallgarth Farm, which overlooks Little Langdale Tarn, are heaps of slate – the spoil from a tiny local quarry, and the very material that the farmhouse itself is made from. Low Hallgarth has the low-pitched slate roof typical of the area.

Opposite: Low Tilberthwaite Farm and Tilberthwaite Cottages in the northern part of Beatrix Potter's Monk Coniston property.

Above: Low Hallgarth Farm in Little Langdale. Spoil heaps are visible above the buildings.

Above: A view of High
Tilberthwaite Farm.

BEATRIX POTTER'S **LAKE DISTRICT**

There is a circular walk from Little Langdale Tarn to this farm, High Tilberthwaite, and back along the opposite side of the valley, that Beatrix must have known well, for it links many of the farms, properties and land she bought as part of the Monk Coniston Estate. The route leads steeply up from the long, low farmhouse of Low Hallgarth, through the leftovers of slate quarries to open moor, then drops, suddenly, to Tilberthwaite and a hidden high valley enclosed by the high slopes of rugged hills. The track leads past her great-grandfather Crompton's Holme Ground Farm, dark, deep quarries, and Stang End Farm with its galleried barn, and then back to Little Langdale.

FARMING

Farming in the Lake District

Rock and mountain, thin soils, high rainfall and long winters determine the size and scope of the Lake District farms. This is sheep-farming country and the farms are essentially small-scale, tucked into the side of a hill above the valley floor and below the harsh mountain land. Beatrix Potter bought fifteen farms in her lifetime, together with the resident flocks of sheep. Farm and flock would then be let to a tenant farmer. She was very much involved in the management of the land and property, and chose her tenants with care. Today the farmers on her land have to apply to the National Trust for tenancy and be interviewed by a National Trust expert. Beatrix stipulated that the Trust should find good tenants and charge them a fair rent.

Beatrix's life span from the mid 1860s to the 1940s covered a period of enormous change in farming. Sheep farmers couldn't compete with cheap imports of wool and refrigerated meat from America, Australia and Argentina. The 1920s were a particular low point, and in 1930 Beatrix bemoaned the fact that the price of fleeces had dropped 'by more than half and still no buyers', and that the local grocer stocked cheap bacon from Poland.

'Mrs Heelis would see her farms as much less interesting today,' believes the local National Trust farming officer. In her time they would have had a mix of sheep, some arable land, and farmyard animals – cows, poultry, pigs – to provide food for local tables, he explained. Farming today is more intensive and specialized, no longer a bit of everything. Today, many farms have been abandoned, and others have part-time farmers who supplement their income with other jobs.

Previous page and above: Views of Eskdale Farm, west of Coniston, below the dizzying heights of Hardknott Pass. The small enclosures, or intakes, around the farm are where cattle may graze and sheep are gathered when they come down from the fell.

Opposite: High Loanthwaite Farm, below the Old Man of Coniston, is on low-lying land where the best soil and sweetest grass is found. Outgangs (tracks linking farm and fell) lead to larger areas of rough grazing in the 'intakes' on the valley wall, and then on to the open fell, where sheep roam freely on tough, wiry grass.

Above and opposite:
Pictures from the National Trust Archive show a horse and cart at Monk Coniston, and horse-drawn ploughs in Borrowdale.

At the turn of the twentieth century there would have been more people and horses working the fields around Sawrey and the Newlands Valley. There was more cultivated ground, and, before the advent of artificial fertilizers and animal feed supplements, flower-rich hay meadows flourished. The arable land was tilled by horse-drawn ploughs; tractors did not replace horses until after the Second World War.

The well-worn look of the fells today is the result of being grazed to the bone. Before the Second World War, the number of grazing stock a farmer had was limited by the distance a shepherd could cover on foot and the capacity of the fell to feed his sheep. Now there are quad bikes and food supplements. Previously woodlands were jointly managed, their timber and fuel recognized as a finite resource. Now there are fewer people around to care. Post-war Government subsidies helped protect farmers from cheap imports, but as they were paid per head of stock, farmers increased the number of animals – and the land became over-grazed. Native heather and juniper were cut back to encourage tough wiry grass, creating a monoculture that left the fells species-poor, exposed, and vulnerable to landslip and erosion.

Opposite: An early twentieth-century farmer gathers his flock of Herdwicks in for marking at Birk Howe Farm, Little Langdale.

Above and left: A modern shepherd with his dog. A quad bike is a convenient means of covering large areas of fell. Livestock roaming free on the open fell must be checked, walls between cultivated and grazed areas maintained, valley drainage systems monitored: all tasks that are traditionally shared between the farmers who use the land.

Right: A painting by Beatrix of sheep in a meadow in snow, entitled 'Winter'.

Opposite: Kirkstone Pass, with a drystone wall cutting across the snow-covered landscape.

Right: Drystone walls, though man-made, are part of the land, for they are built with stones from the ground they stand on. The rounded pebbles in the wall were tumble-smoothed in the fast-moving meltwater of a great glacier. Big foundation rocks embedded in turf at the base are a clue that a wall is very old – maybe two hundred and fifty years. The chunks of rock get smaller higher up the wall, and are anchored by coping stones that run right through to the other side.

Snow may lie on the high fells for eight months of the year, although this is rare, as the Lake District climate is generally maritime, moist and moderate. Mountains like these, at the Kirkstone Pass above Beatrix's Troutbeck Park Estate, are like great walls that channel the weather, providing shelter to some valleys and creating wind tunnels or dumping places for rain in others. Borrowdale, for example, is the wettest inhabited place in the British Isles. Just a few miles away, though, Keswick, has less than a third of Borrowdale's rainfall, and, in her letters from Sawrey, Beatrix occasionally complained of summer drought. In a given year, gales may scour the mountain tops for a hundred days, while sheltered valleys may only have five days of gale-force wind.

Herdwick sheep are the only breed that can consistently survive winter on the Lake District fells. There are no boundaries on the open fell; the sheep are 'heafed', that is, they learn from being shepherded for generations where their boundaries are and know where to head at lambing time.

Only the tups (rams) have horns. The Herdwick breed are of sturdier build than lowland sheep and take longer to develop, so farmers have to wait longer before a ewe is ready to lamb at three years old. Slow-maturing animals need few nutrients, which is why Herdwicks can thrive on the cheap and readily available low-nutrient grazing of the fells.

Herdwick ewes are gathered into the in-bye (fields by the farm) for mating in the autumn, lambing in March and for dipping and shearing in high summer. In between times they roam freely on the open fell. Lambs are weaned in October and sold on to be 'finished off' – fattened up on a lowland farm for a couple of months. The only problem is that Herdwicks who have been raised on the wiry fell grass often refuse to eat rich feed supplements.

A farmer clips one kilogram of wool from a Herdwick sheep compared with two to three kilograms from a lowland breed such as a Swaledale. The wool used to be burnt as wastage because the labour and transport cost more than the wool could be sold for. It is coarse and grey, and its short length made spinning difficult.

In recent times, however, the determination of David Townsend, National Trust Herdwick Project Officer, has persuaded a local carpet manufacturer to produce high quality carpets that are hard-wearing and stain-resistant because of the natural oils in them. The farmers get 50p a kilo for the wool, which just about covers the shearing costs.

Traditionally, Lake District farmers kept cattle for their manure and to keep the grass sweet, but today cattle stock is declining, limited to a few small dairy farms that supply produce for local consumption. There has been a trend for Lakeland farmers to buy in continental breeds of cattle but these need shelter and extra feed, and generally lack the stamina and survival ability of indigenous highland breeds such as red-haired longhorns.

IN TRUST FOR THE NATION

In trust for the nation

The 'natural' beauty of the Lakeland mountains and the cameos of countryside in Beatrix Potter's tales owe as much to human intervention as they do to nature. Broad-leaved woodland once covered all but the highest and most waterlogged land. Then, around 1,500 years ago, hill farming became established, and the wholesale felling of trees for grazing, clearings and settlements transformed the landscape. Over the centuries, a unique Lake District ecosystem developed, created by a balance of natural and human forces.

Beatrix Heelis died over sixty years ago, in December 1943, but she had long been aware of the threats facing the Lake District countryside and the way of life it sustained. She had bought land and property with the intention of leaving it to the National Trust, the organization co-founded by her old friend Hardwicke Rawnsley in 1895. The Trust's purpose is to acquire countryside and property of cultural importance, and literally hold it in trust for the nation: to protect and preserve it, and make it available for everyone to enjoy. 'The Trust,' Beatrix wrote in 1932, 'is a noble thing, and – humanly speaking – immortal.' She was giving clear instructions to the Trust as to how she wanted things to be managed on her property as early as 1926, but maintained an active and lively interest herself, until she died seventeen years later. On her death she left over 4,000 acres of land to the National Trust. But during her lifetime, she gave the Trust another valuable gift: the benefit of her experience in managing land and property. She 'brought vision, determination and extraordinary generosity to the Trust', wrote Merlin Waterson in his history of the National Trust.

It is now the National Trust's job to ensure that the land, the cottages, farmhouses and other properties bequeathed to them are conserved and enjoyed as Beatrix intended. Their challenge is to achieve the right balance between the different land uses and demands on the countryside, and to ensure that no single element becomes invasive. The regional officers for the Lake District National Trust today talk about Beatrix Heelis with tremendous respect; and they believe they understand what she wanted. 'Mrs Heelis was a realist; she didn't stand still, and she wouldn't want us to.'

Above: Hill Top Farm and Near Sawrey today.

Opposite, above and below: Filming *Miss Potter* on location in the Lake District.

Right: Miss Potter (Renée Zellweger) stands in front of her farmhouse. The location of the real Hill Top Farm was unsuitable for a film set and so for the purposes of the film another of Beatrix Potter's properties, Yew Tree Farm (seen here), was transformed into a Hill Top look-alike.

Hill Top Farm in Sawrey is, as Beatrix wished, just as she left it, full of her treasures and country furniture, and of scenes that appear in the tales. It is one of the most popular tourist spots in the Lake District, and opening times are limited in an attempt to reduce wear and tear.

The newly released film *Miss Potter*, starring the American actress Renée Zellweger, will not only perpetuate the legend of Beatrix Potter but also add to the Lake District's annual twelve million day visits by tourists. Beatrix Potter's legacy to the National Trust is double-edged: her fame attracts the very forces that damage the land she was so passionate about protecting.

Many farms need to supplement their income by offering accommodation. Beatrix recognized that providing amenities for tourists helped preserve the continuance of traditional ways of life and farming. She wrote of Yew Tree Farm, 'The farm can hardly pay without the teas and visitors.' Today, Yew Tree is a model of sustainable farming and land use. In addition to the tea rooms, it offers bed and breakfast accommodation, and has a 'white room', licensed to sell meat from the Herdwick sheep direct from the farm by mail order.

Containing tourists within designated camping areas reduces wear and risk of fire from camping wild. Mrs Heelis suggested to the National Trust having fixed sites in 1931. Scouts and guides were likely to care for the land, 'but the public in general are not . . . Promiscuous choosing of sites by campers . . . won't do at all.'

'It is to the good that there should be this new widespread interest in the overworked word "amenity",' Beatrix wrote to the widow of Canon Hardwicke Rawnsley in 1934. The trick is to encourage visitors who bring much-needed income to the area, without harming the environment. 'We want more visitors who respect the place,' explains one of the National Trust wardens. The lakes themselves provide a large variety of activities for visitors.

Left: Beyond an array of canoes, visitors queue to embark on a pleasure boat on Derwentwater.

Opposite below: Rowing on Windermere.

Below: Wind-surfing. on Derwentwater

IN TRUST FOR THE NATION

In 1935 Beatrix reported 'serious trouble with motorcycles' on ancient footpaths. Today, even walking, in what is one of Britain's most popular hiking areas, causes problems. The tread of a million hiking boots has eroded a 12ft (4m) gully on one mountain path. As a signed-up member of a local footpath association, Beatrix would be delighted in the recent three million pound grant from the National Lottery which will fund the next five years of the National Trust's footpath protection programme.

Over-intensive grazing by too many animals has denuded the fells of protective vegetation. Steep slopes denuded of vegetation are vulnerable to erosion and landslip; plants can act as a brake to material running off from the mountains and building up as sediment in the lakes. The Trust believes that the numbers of livestock grazing fells such Caudale Head, opposite, need to be reduced by half to two thirds, for the right balance to be achieved. Moorland shrubs and trees such as sessile oak, juniper and heather will then have a chance to re-establish.

Opposite: The bare, over-grazed fells below Caudale Head, east of Kirkstone Pass.

Above left: Scafell Pike Trail was built by National Trust teams in rough stones.

Above right: Stone paths are laid so that as little erosion as possible occurs.

Left: An area of moorland just above Moss Eccles Tarn, near Sawrey, has been enclosed to keep grazing animals out. Four years on, junipers that had been nibbled back to their rootstock are making a come-back and a greater diversity of grass species is evident. Diversity leads to a balanced ecosystem.

There are probably fewer hedges and stone walls than when Beatrix Potter bought her first farm at the beginning of the twentieth century. Hedges harbour a rich variety of wildlife and contribute to the biodiversity of the countryside. But they need to be maintained and not bulldozed away to be replaced by non-biodegradable fencing.

The mosses and lichens that grow on the stone walls and boulders in the damp atmosphere are evidence that the air is still unpolluted.

Water is another matter, however. Esthwaite has a tranquil and perfect beauty on a calm spring morning, and yet the lake of Mr Jeremy Fisher is seriously polluted by untreated sewerage from Hawkshead and chemical run-off from farms. Feed from a trout farm has altered the natural balance of nutrients. Sometimes the lake is covered in algae, which blocks oxygen, and a variety of plant and animal species have been lost. The National Trust intends to tackle the lake's environmental problems: 'We want to get the balance right as it was in Mrs Heelis's day,' commented a National Trust warden.

Opposite above: An award-winning hedge on Low Sizergh Farm, which is part of the Soil Association Organic Farm Network.

Opposite below: Thick green moss grows on rocks in Strutta Wood near Ashness Bridge, Borrowdale, evidence of a clean atmosphere.

Above: Esthwaite Water, clean in Beatrix's day, was her favourite of all the lakes and she painted it in all seasons.

Left: Signs on the banks of the lakes prohibit drinking water.

Regional National Trust officers have replaced Beatrix in managing her farms and estates. The farms are let out to tenants, who are carefully vetted as Beatrix had requested. Some are on old tenancy agreements that have passed down through three generations. The Trust is replacing these with short-term lets that can include clauses to give a greater level of protection, such as stipulating the amount of artificial fertilizer or maximum number of grazing stock.

Some local people felt that the National Trust had betrayed Beatrix Heelis's wishes in closing down High Yewdale as a working farm, but the Trust believes she would have taken similar action. 'Mrs Heelis wanted to preserve traditions but she was also astute and forward-looking. The figures at Yewdale didn't add up. The land was split between three separate farms, and we decided to amalgamate it, just as Mrs Heelis did with Hill Top and Castle Farm, to make them a more viable unit. At one of the farms we are converting the barns into craft workshops. Most of the local farms have more buildings than they need.'

Beatrix requested that the local Herdwick sheep continue to be the resident breed on her hill farms. Many Herdwicks had to be slaughtered in the foot-and-mouth epidemic of 2001, and with them the ingrained memory of heafing was lost. Heafing is the instinctive knowledge of their territorial limits in the open fell, that is passed down from one generation to another. New herds have had to re-heaf, or re-learn – initially with the help of electric fencing. The positive news for the Herdwick breed is that new markets are being found for their meat, and eighty per cent of their wool now produces high quality carpets.

Left: Belmount House, north of Hawkshead.

Above: The rocking chair at Hill Top originally came from Belmount.

As well as general care for the environment, the National Trust has an important requirement to maintain the numerous individual places of beauty or historical interest which are in its possession. Belmount House, a gracious Georgian building close to Wray, was bought by Beatrix and passed on to the National Trust. She requested in her will that the big walled garden be preserved as a bird sanctuary. The Trust has also carefully renovated the house, which has many original features such as moulded coving.

Beatrix was as interested in preserving old, finely crafted and traditional furniture as she was in the properties she bought. Often a property was sold together with much of its original, sometimes fitted, oak-carved furniture. Other items were 'riven out of ancestral cottages', bought by Beatrix at local auctions, and given a new home in one of her properties. The rocking chair at Hill Top is American; it came from Rebecca Owen, who lived at Belmount House.

Above: The exterior of the Heelis offices.

Above right: The pigeon-hole sorting rack in the entrance room.

Right and opposite: William Heelis's office is furnished as it would have been in his day, with a period telephone and typewriter, papers on the desk, and golf clubs in the corner.

The offices of William Heelis & Sons, solicitors, where Beatrix and William had founded their relationship, have been meticulously preserved by the National Trust. William died less than two years after his wife, and left the property to the nation on the understanding that resident solicitors could stay there for as long as they needed. Walls have been restored with lathe and plaster and coloured with lime-wash from traditional recipes; oak panelling is fixed with specially made oak pegs, and any necessary adaptations for the building's current use as the Beatrix Potter Gallery are reversible. The upstairs rooms contain an annually changing selection of Beatrix Potter's original watercolours, book illustrations and manuscripts.

The memorial stone in Brandelhow Park reads:

BRANDELHOW
THE FIRST PROPERTY OF THE
NATIONAL TRUST IN THIS DISTRICT
WAS OPENED ON 16TH OCTOBER 1902 BY
H.R.H. THE PRINCESS LOUISE
FOUR OAKS WERE PLANTED HERE BY
PRINCESS LOUISE
MISS OCTAVIA HILL
SIR ROBERT HUNTER
CANON H.D. RAWNSLEY

Above top: The memorial stone in Brandelhow Park, commemorating the first National Trust acquisition in the Lake District.

Above: Beech trees in Brandelhow Park.

Right: The 'Hundred Year Stone' sculpted by Peter Randall-Page to commemorate the National Trust Centenary.

Brandelhow Park, on the westward shores of Derwentwater, was the result of the National Trust's first major appeal for funds to buy land, in 1902, and a stone commemorates the event. [The land] 'will be preserved in its present loveliness and it belongs to you all and to every landless man, woman and child in England,' Octavia Hill, founding member of the Trust, told an Oxford audience at the time.

A glacial boulder sculpted by Peter Randall-Page commemorates the centenary of the National Trust in 1995, and is at Broomhill Point, Derwentwater.

The cabochon-smooth gem of Tarn Hows catches the colour of the changing skies, and waves of fells roll away in every direction. This not quite natural beauty spot was enhanced by its early nineteenth-century owners to create the Victorian ideal of a romantic landscape. The basin of land in which it lies was dammed to create a single lake in the place of three small tarns, and native deciduous trees and conifers

BEATRIX POTTER'S **LAKE DISTRICT**

were planted. With particular attention to detail, horses were used to pull timber out for minimum impact on the land. Its conservation was ensured when the Monk Coniston Estate passed to the National Trust on Beatrix Potter's death. The National Trust aim to restore the scene to what its Victorian owners intended, and improve access and facilities for tourists – with the help of a Heritage Lottery Fund.

IN TRUST FOR THE NATION

'I do not remember a time when I did not try to invent pictures and make for myself a fairyland amongst the wild flowers, the animals, fungi, mosses, woods and streams, all the thousand objects of the countryside; that pleasant, unchanging world of realism and romance, which in our northern clime is stiffened by hard weather, a tough ancestry, and the strength that comes from the hills,' wrote Beatrix towards the end of her life.

Today you can gaze over the same views that Beatrix captured in her paintings, and if you explore the high fells, the spinneys and rolling fields, or the damp woodlands on the lake shores, it is largely thanks to her that much of it is still there to be enjoyed.

Above: Grasmere with mist rising on the far shore

Index

Page references for illustrations are in *italics*

Above: A river running through the Buttermere Valley

Acknowledgements

The publishers would like to thank the staff at the National Trust for their help during the preparation of this book. Particular thanks are due to John Stachiewicz, Chris Lacey, Liz Hunter and John Moffat for assistance in supplying information and material.

The photographs and illustrations are reproduced by kind permission of the following copyright holders (listed by page number):

Armitt Trust 114 (below)
Alex Bailey 164 (below), 165 (above, centre and below)
Beatrix Potter Society 16 (right)
Gilly Cameron Cooper 22, 32 (above and below), 34 (above and below), 37 (below), 42, 54, 59 (above right), 111 (below), 154 (below), 171 (below)
Frederick Warne Archive 44 (above), 46, 52, 100 (below)
iStockphoto/Gary Forsyth 43 (below)
Trustees of the Linder Collection 16 (left), 33 (above and below right), 47, 49 (below right), 53 (above left and right), 57 (above left), 70, 98 (right), 135 (below)
National Trust 19, 28, 44 (below left), 50 (above), 53 (below), 57 (above right), 75 (below right), 100 (above), 121 (above), 130 (above right), 134 (below), 135 (above left), 185 (left)
National Trust Picture Library 49 (below left), 150, 151, 152
National Trust Picture Library/Matthew Antrobus 137 (right), 138
National Trust Picture Library/Niall Benvie 51
National Trust Picture Library/Alex Black 113
National Trust Picture Library/Val Corbett 130 (above left), 158, 166 (above and below), 181
National Trust Picture Library/Joe Cornish 2, 6, 12–13, 15, 20–1, 29 (above), 30, 38–9, 41 (below), 43 (above), 45, 56, 58, 59 (above left), 60 (above right), 61, 64, 65, 66, 67 (below), 68–9, 75 (above), 95 (above), 96, 101, 105, 106, 108–9, 110 (left), 119, 120, 121 (below), 123 (right), 124 (above left), 126–7, 129, 139 (above), 141, 142, 143, 144–5, 149, 155, 156, 157 (above and below), 159, 163, 164 (above), 167, 170, 171 (above left and right), 174, 175, 176, 180 (above left), 182–3, 184

National Trust Picture Library/Derek Croucher 9, 180 (below left)
National Trust Picture Library/John Darley 67 (above)
National Trust Picture Library/Geoffrey Frosh 77 (above left), 78 (right), 79, 80 (right), 81 (above), 82 (below), 83, 84 (below left)
National Trust Picture Library/Lee Frost 40–1, 48–9, 114–15, 172 (below)
National Trust Picture Library/Derek Harris 55
National Trust Picture Library/Roger Hickman 5
National Trust Picture Library/David Levenson 102–3, 131, 153 (above and below), 172 (above)
National Trust Picture Library/Anthony Marshall 115 (below), 186–7
National Trust Picture Library/Leo Mason 168–9 (all)
National Trust Picture Library/Nick Meers 116–17
National Trust Picture Library/John Miller 136
National Trust Picture Library/David Noton 36, 62–3, 62 (below), 63 (below), 122, 146–7, 148, 160–1, 188–9, 190–1
National Trust Picture Library/T. J. Rich 132
National Trust Picture Library/Kevin Richardson 140
National Trust Picture Library/Stephen Robson 71, 73, 86, 88, 90 (above left), 91, 92–3 (all)
National Trust Picture Library/Simon Upton 76, 78 (below left), 80 (below left), 82 (above), 84 (above left and right), 85 (above and below), 134 (above), 177 (right), 178 (above right and below, 179)
National Trust Picture Library/Ian West 125 (above)
National Trust Picture Library/Mike Williams 118 (below)
Dan Newman 24–5, 27 (above and below), 37 (above), 75 (below left), 88 (above and below right), 95 (below left), 97 (above right), 98 (below left), 99 (above), 110 (below right), 111 (above), 112 (above right), 173 (below), 178 (above left)
Private Collectors 18 (right), 24 (below), 33 (below right), 35 (above and below), 94 (left)
Victoria and Albert Museum 14, 17, 18 (left), 23, 26, 29 (below), 31 (above), 44 (centre), 60 (below), 107 (above), 118 (above), 135 (above right), 154 (above), 173 (above)